P9-DHT-054

The Poetic Art of
ROBERT LOWELL

Grinnel
Book

The Poetic Art of
ROBERT LOWELL

Marjorie G. Perloff

Cornell University Press | ITHACA AND LONDON

Copyright © 1973 by Cornell University

All rights reserved. Except for brief quotations in a review, this book, or parts thereof, must not be reproduced in any form without permission in writing from the publisher. For information address Cornell University Press, 124 Roberts Place, Ithaca, New York 14850.

First published 1973 by Cornell University Press.
Published in the United Kingdom by Cornell University Press Ltd., 2–4 Brook Street, London W1Y 1AA.

Quotations are reprinted with the permission of Farrar, Straus & Giroux, Inc., and Faber & Faber, Ltd., from the following titles by Robert Lowell: *For the Union Dead*, copyright © 1956, 1960, 1961, 1962, 1963, 1964 by Robert Lowell; *Life Studies*, copyright © 1956, 1959 by Robert Lowell; *Near the Ocean*, copyright © 1963, 1965, 1966, 1967 by Robert Lowell; *Imitations*, copyright © 1958, 1959, 1960, 1961 by Robert Lowell; *Notebook 1967–68*, copyright © 1967, 1968, 1969 by Robert Lowell; *Notebook*, copyright © 1967, 1968, 1969, 1970 by Robert Lowell; and from *Love & Fame* by John Berryman, copyright © 1970 by John Berryman.

Quotations are reprinted by permission of Faber and Faber, Ltd., from *Poems 1938–1949* by Robert Lowell.

The quotation from "The Longing" by Theodore Roethke, copyright © 1962 by Beatrice Roethke, administratrix of the estate of Theodore Roethke, from *The Collected Poems of Theodore Roethke*, is reprinted by permission of Doubleday & Company, Inc., and Faber & Faber, Ltd.

"The Stones" by Sylvia Plath, from *The Colossus and Other Poems* by Sylvia Plath (Alfred A. Knopf, New York; Faber & Faber, London), copyright © 1960, 1962 by Sylvia Plath, copyright © 1967 by Ted Hughes, is reprinted by permission of Alfred A. Knopf, Inc., and Olwyn Hughes.

"Mémoire" by Arthur Rimbaud and the translation by Wallace Fowlie are reprinted from *Rimbaud: Complete Works*, edited and translated by Wallace Fowlie, by permission of The University of Chicago Press, copyright © 1966, 1967 by Wallace Fowlie.

Excerpts from *Lord Weary's Castle* and *The Mills of the Kavanaughs* are reprinted by permission of Harcourt Brace Jovanovich, Inc.; copyright 1946, 1947, 1948, 1951 by Robert Lowell.

International Standard Book Number 0-8014-0771-0
Library of Congress Catalog Card Number 72-12412

Printed in the United States of America by Vail-Ballou Press, Inc.

Librarians: Library of Congress cataloging information appears on the last page of the book.

B+T
12-4-73
9.50

To my mother and father:

ILSE and MAXIMILIAN MINTZ

Copy 1

Contents

Preface

Although Robert Lowell is held by many to be the out-standing poet writing in English in the period since World War II, there is little agreement about the nature of his achievement or the permanent value of his poetry. The recent *Notebook* (1970), for example, has been alternately hailed as "Lowell's best volume since *Life Studies*" [1] and deplored as a hastily written and "depressing" book, in which the poet has "surrendered . . . forlornly to self-parody, the strenuous but machine-like animation of dead mannerisms." [2] If there is no consensus on the poet's work, it is probably because Lowell criticism has tended to be either casually impressionistic on the one hand or insistently explicative on the other. Thanks to such scholars as Hugh Staples, Jerome Mazzaro, Phillip Cooper, and Richard J. Fein, we now know pretty well what the more difficult Lowell poems mean, what sources the poet uses, and to what myths, historical events, or Biblical texts he alludes. But explication can never take us far enough; as Lowell himself said in a symposium on Stanley Kunitz: "Analysis is necessary for teaching poems, and for student papers. Still, somehow, nothing very fresh or to the point is said. One knows ahead of time how the machine will grind. . . . There is even a kind of modern poem, now produced in bulk, that seems written to be explained." [3]

In the pages that follow, I have accordingly slighted both

ix

poem-by-poem explication and general discussion of Lowell's politics, religion, or social thought in favor of the description and evaluation of such purely literary aspects of the poetry as imagery, genre, convention, syntax, and tone. Like Stevens' "Thirteen Ways of Looking at a Blackbird," my six chapters all treat the same object—Lowell's lyric poetry— but each views it from a different perspective and raises different, though related, questions. The underlying aim has been to discriminate, as carefully as possible, between what is permanently valuable in Lowell's poetry and what is second-rate. This is no easy matter for, although Lowell's poetic vision is, as I shall argue, astonishingly consistent and coherent, his work is extremely uneven in technical execution.

I begin with a detailed examination of Lowell's imagery. The opening chapter classifies and discusses the major recurrent images in the poetry in an attempt to define, in its main outlines, the structure of Lowell's universe. This chapter could not have been written without the example of the great French phenomenologist critic Jean-Pierre Richard, whose essays on the poetry of Nerval, Baudelaire, and Rimbaud in *Poésie et Profondeur* first suggested to me a viable method of exploring the contours of Lowell's imaginative landscape.

From his earliest Catholic poetry to the skeptical sonnets of *Notebook* and the new *Dolphin* series, Lowell draws his images from the same areas of experience and relates them in similar ways. But such consistency paradoxically becomes a drawback when the poet tries to merge his voice with those of the great poets of the past, as Lowell does in his "imitations." Chapter Two takes up this problem: I examine the genre of the imitations, specifically those of Rimbaud, in order to see what happens when the oracular, ecstatic, and visionary mode of a Rimbaud is domesticated by the historical and essentially realistic consciousness of a Robert Lowell.

In Chapter Three, my aim is to define and to evaluate the

so-called confessional mode inaugurated by the famous *Life Studies* poems. *Life Studies* is, I believe, Lowell's central achievement; nothing the poet has written either before or after this volume matches its delicacy of tone, its artful structure, its highly original conjunction of verse and prose. Accordingly, when I discuss Lowell's syntax in Chapter Four, I again take *Life Studies* as my point of departure, and then move back to the earlier *Lord Weary's Castle* and forward to *Notebook* to determine to what degree syntax becomes an index to the larger poetic value of a given work.

Chapters Three and Four are largely formalistic studies; I have been influenced here by the Russian formalists, particularly Roman Jakobson, as well as by Leo Spitzer's great studies on stylistics. The methodology used in Chapter Four is based, to some degree, on that of Josephine Miles's important study, *Eras and Modes in English Poetry,* as well as on Helen Vendler's brilliant analysis of Wallace Stevens' syntax, in *On Extended Wings: Wallace Stevens' Longer Poems.*

The fifth chapter is both more thematically oriented than the earlier ones and more critical of Lowell's achievement. The manipulation of the speaking voice has always been, I believe, Lowell's greatest artistic problem. In tracing the development of tone in the "Winslow" elegies—the series of elegies to his Winslow or maternal relatives—I have come to the conclusion that only in his middle period, the period of *Life Studies* and *For the Union Dead,* has Lowell been entirely successful in distancing and objectifying his lyric "I." In a general way, this chapter owes a debt to Irvin Ehrenpreis' widely reprinted essay, "The Age of Lowell," which I have found to be the most helpful piece of criticism on Lowell's poetry to date. Chapter Five is the only one in which I refer extensively to what other critics have said of Lowell, if only to disagree with some of their overly enthusiastic evaluations of the early poetry and of the latest work.

In the Conclusion, finally, my aim is to view Lowell's

characteristic poetic style against the background of contemporary poetry. After a close analysis of "Waking in the Blue," in which I sum up the findings of my earlier chapters, I compare "Waking" to similar poems in the same genre— that of the "mental hospital poem"—by two of Lowell's leading contemporaries, John Berryman and Sylvia Plath. Such comparison raises some interesting questions as to Lowell's probable future influence.

Because my main interest is in the nature of poetic form and genre, I have not attempted complete coverage of Lowell's writings. The plays, for example, raise complex issues that fall outside the scope of this study, and certain volumes of poetry—*The Mills of the Kavanaughs* and *Near the Ocean*—are neglected in favor of those that are pivotal in Lowell's development. There are really two central questions to which this book addresses itself: what *kind* of poetry does Lowell write? and what is its *value?* I hope that others will be prompted to continue and to enlarge upon the discussion of these difficult and challenging problems.

Anyone writing on Robert Lowell must be grateful to Hugh Staples, whose *Robert Lowell: The First Twenty Years* (1962) contains an excellent bibliography of Lowell's writings through *Life Studies* (1959), and to Jerome Mazzaro, whose "Checklist 1939–1968" in *Robert Lowell: A Portrait of the Artist in His Time* (1970), edited by Michael London and Robert Boyers, is an indispensable source for biographical and critical material on Lowell.

My readings of Lowell's poetry have benefited from conversations with Evelyn T. Beck, Milne Holton, Norma Procopiow, James Hafley, Susan Anthony, and especially with my husband, Joseph K. Perloff, with whom I discussed the manuscript at every stage, and who gave me invaluable suggestions and support.

I am especially grateful to William H. Rueckert of the

University of Rochester, who read the manuscript with great care and offered invaluable suggestions for revisions and additions.

My greatest debt is to my friend and former colleague at Catholic University, Gerda Blumenthal, who offered me the benefit of her superb insights into literature and of her wide knowledge of contemporary continental criticism.

I am grateful to Joyce Handley and Sharon Landolt, both of the University of Maryland, who patiently typed the manuscript, and to Camoline Gales and Catherine Sullivan, who freed me from many household duties so that I could find the time to write.

I am grateful to the University of Maryland for a General Research Board Award for the summer of 1972, which helped me to see the manuscript through its final stages.

Portions of Chapters Three and Five have appeared as articles. I am grateful for permission to reprint, with some changes, "Death by Water: The Winslow Elegies of Robert Lowell," *English Literary History*, 34 (1967), 116–140, © The Johns Hopkins Press; and "Realism and the Confessional Mode of Robert Lowell," *Contemporary Literature*, 11 (copyright © 1970 by the Regents of the University of Wisconsin), 470–487.

MARJORIE G. PERLOFF

College Park, Maryland

Abbreviations

The Poetic Art of
ROBERT LOWELL

Chapter One

"The Unforgivable Landscape": The Nexus of Images

One dark night
my Tudor Ford climbed the hill's skull;
I watched for love-cars. Lights turned down,
they lay together, hull to hull,
where the graveyard shelves on the town.
"Skunk Hour"

The "One dark night" of "Skunk Hour"—the painful moment of terror and anxiety that leads to a renewal of self-insight and understanding—this is the central experience which Lowell's self undergoes. The scene of the poem is the "hill's skull," a reference that immediately suggests Calvary and death, and the poet's vantage point is that contemporary monster, the automobile, here ironically bearing the absurd brand name of "Tudor [pun on two-door] "Ford." The "love cars" for which the poet neurotically watches in his isolation imperceptibly turn into grounded ships and then into coffins: those who lie together in this strangely distorted world are not human beings but inanimate objects. Lovers' lane is no longer an idyllic pastoral retreat; it is located "where the graveyard shelves on the town." Graveyard and city are indeed one and the same place.

Surely no other contemporary poet has given us so loving and palpable a recreation of the quixotic relationship between the modern sensibility, simultaneously haunted by the past and acutely sensitive to the present, and the social and physical environment in which that sensibility must func-

tion. Long before ecologists began to declaim about our polluted rivers, our unlivable cities, and our monstrous technol-
ogy, Lowell was drawing verbal maps of eroding hillsides
and urban sprawl. Like the characters of Chekhov, one of his
acknowledged masters,[1] Lowell's personae respond to their
puzzling environment with a mixture of pathos, irony, disgust, and humor. The greatest pleasure in reading Lowell's
poetry is perhaps that of recognition. The name "Tudor
Ford," for example, epitomizes for the reader the preten-
tiousness and vulgarity of the modern sensibility that longs
for a perfect combination of streamlined efficiency and old-
world glamor.

The consistency and coherence of Lowell's imaginative
cosmos have often been questioned.[2] Lowell's early poetry,
we are told, is Catholic and apocalyptic; its language and
verse forms are conventional and formal; its images are
drawn from the liturgy, the Bible, Greek mythology, Roman
history. *Life Studies* (1959) is the great watershed: written
after Lowell's break with the Church, the new poetry is informal and autobiographical; its diction is casual and colloquial, its sound patterns tend to be almost prosaic. Yet
Lowell himself insisted in his *Paris Review* interview that
the vision of *Life Studies* was not essentially different from
that of *Lord Weary's Castle* (1947): "I don't feel my experience changed very much. . . . It's very much the same struggle, light and darkness, the flux of experience. The morality
seems much the same." [3]

Undoubtedly, Lowell's style has undergone marked
changes in the last two decades—changes I shall consider in
later chapters. But when one examines the recurrent images
in Lowell's poetry, one is astonished by the peculiar consistency of the poet's vision. In this chapter I propose to describe, as precisely as possible, the pervasive imaginative
structure of Lowell's poetic world. If we discount those images that play a role in only an isolated volume or set of
poems—for example, the Marian imagery in *Land of Un-*

likeness (1944) and *Lord Weary's Castle,* the repeated references to decor in *Life Studies,* or the food and liquor imagery in *Notebook 1967–68*—the recurrent images in
Lowell's poetry can be seen to fall into three basic categories: the natural world—the world of violent seasons,
blighted vegetation, and trapped animals; the social and psychological landscape in which man dwells—the world of
noise, speed, and pollution, whose symbol is the automobile
and whose terminus is the hospital, the prison, or the graveyard; and the historical or human landscape in which the
self struggles for fulfillment—the world of time, place, and
person.

Much of the thematic tension in Lowell's poetry is gener-
ated by the conflict between this third group of images (persons and places in particular time sequences) and the other
two. It is the recreation of a particular sensibility (usually
but not always the poet's own self) undergoing a revelatory
experience that compensates, at least to a degree, for the
sense of death conveyed by both the nature imagery and the
picture of the psychological and social climate of the modern
world. "My night," Lowell said of "Skunk Hour," "is not
gracious, but secular, puritan, and agnostical. An Existentialist night." [4] This is a very just remark. Rimbaud called his
great autobiographical poem written in 1873, "Une saison en
enfer." For Lowell's self, born almost a century later, all seasons are spent in hell. The only questions that remain, therefore, are, in the words of Wallace Stevens, "How to live.
What to do."

The World of Nature

> I saw the sky descending, black and white,
> Not blue, on Boston.
> "Where the Rainbow Ends"

For Lowell, the "earth choking its tears" is a shrunken
planet, whose topography is no more than the externaliza-

tion of the poet's inner landscape. No fountains or streams nourish the self. The "rain weeps in darkness" or "whips the air," and when illumination does come, it is too violent to bear: "armfuls of lightning / crash on the . . . cottage / to smash it with light" (*Imit*, 138–139). In this urbanized version of Eliot's Waste Land, the flowers have withered and the birds departed, leaving behind scarred fields and cement piles, inhabited by stray cats, rodents, and petty insects. The sheer ugliness of Lowell's valley of ashes is all but unrelieved.

The Two Seasons. In Lowell's world, April is no longer the cruelest month; it has merely ceased to exist. The sky— whether over Boston, New York, or Buenos Aires—can never be perceived as *blue,* for in the poet's imagination it is always January or the Fourth of July. As soon as the "shifting snow" (*LWC,* 17) and "cindered ice" (*LWC,* 4) melt, turning into "muck and winter dropsy" (*LWC,* 23), "skidding summer" (*Nbk,* 22) steams in, bringing an oppressive sun that "never sets upon these hell-fire streets / Of Boston" (*LWC,* 47).[5] The absence of spring and fall—the green and golden seasons—is particularly striking in *Notebook,* in whose "Afterthought" Lowell carefully explains that "The time is a summer, an autumn, a winter, a spring, another summer. . . . My plot rolls with the seasons" (*Nbk,* 262). Despite this insistence on the seasonal cycle as organizing principle, Lowell cannot bring himself to include spring in the sequence; the "April" sonnets (pp. 151–159), for example, present historical and literary vignettes that have nothing to do with the time of year, whereas in the "Midwinter" sequence, the poet visualizes Central Park as a "tundra" in which snow is "mucking to pepper and salt, to brain-cell dull, to ink" and feels that even the freshest snowfall—the "white foam-wisp"—will surely "poison when it hits / the Hudson's prone and essence-steaming back" (*Nbk,* 110, 126).

To perceive the weather as an endless succession of blinding snow storms and oppressive heat waves is to view the outside world as a projection of the self's inner desolation and emptiness. Unlike, say, Wallace Stevens, for whom a bird's "scrawny cry," heard "At the earliest ending of winter," can bring intimations of the "colossal sun" of spring,[6] Lowell is a poet for whom "the season's ill" (*LS*, 89) regardless of the time of year. "All day," muses the speaker of "Winter in Dunbarton," "The wastes of snow about my house stare in / Through idle windows" (*LWC*, 23). "Again and then again . . . the year is born / To ice and death" (*LWC*, 7; spaced dots, Lowell's). The very Swiss Alps, that favorite Romantic symbol of grandeur and spiritual elevation, are viewed by the poet as "backward and wasted," and the Alpine snow is neither white nor sparkling, but "fallow" (*LS*, 3–4). "Inauguration Day: January 1953," a poem which pessimistically compares Eisenhower's future presidency to the misguided leadership of such military heroes as Stuyvesant and Grant, uses a network of cold–snow–ice images to define the "mausoleum" at the very heart of our Republic:

> The snow had buried Stuyvesant.
> The subways drummed the vaults. I heard
> the El's green girders charge on Third,
> Manhattan's truss of adamant,
> that groaned in ermine, slummed on want. . . .
> Cyclonic zero of the word,
> God of our armies, who interred
> Cold Harbor's blue immortals, Grant!
> Horseman, your sword is in the groove!
>
> Ice, ice. Our wheels no longer move.
>   [LS, 7; spaced dots, Lowell's]

When the death of the spirit is not seen, as it is here, in terms of icy tombs, it is associated with the fiery furnace. Summer is "the season / when our friends may and will die

daily" (*FUD*, 64), the season when "the sunlight is a sword /
Striking at the withholder of the Lord" (*LWC*, 47), or when
"the sun's / daily remorseful blackout dawns" (*NO*, 16).
July, America's ostensible "month of freedom," is seen sardonically as the month which "tigerstriped the sky / With
bombs and rockets" (*MK*, 18), while August is associated
with mildew (*LWC*, 58) or drought (*NO*, 46). "Even in August," as Lowell's Anne Kavanaugh puts it, "it was autumn" (*MK*, 20). It is interesting that in Lowell's most recent poems, the *Dolphin* sonnets, in which British lawns and
country houses replace the setting of urban America, the
poet is still disturbed by the "Midday heat" which "draws
poison from the Jacobean brick." [7]

Not only do winter and summer images regularly alternate in Lowell's poetry, but when the poet wishes to empha-
size the isolation and death of the self, he merges the two
clusters. Thus, in "Sailing Home from Rapallo," the poet's
painful journey with his mother's corpse takes him across the
ocean from a sunny Italy where "the whole shoreline of the
Golfo di Genova / was breaking into fiery flower," to the family cemetery at Dunbarton, which "lay under the White
Mountains / in the sub-zero weather." Idly reclining in his
deck chair on the ocean liner, the poet is haunted by the
image of gravestones:

> The burning cold illuminated
> the hewn inscriptions of Mother's relatives:
> twenty or thirty Winslows and Starks.
> Frost had given their names a diamond edge.   [*LS*, 78]

This *burning cold* is death in its most absolute form. The
image recurs in "For the Union Dead," in which "The old
South Boston Aquarium stands / in a Sahara of snow now"
(*FUD*, 70), and in Lowell's imitation of Mallarmé's "Le
Cygne": "the great boredoms blaze in the sterile winter"
(*Nbk*, 133). The poet's season of discontent is thus an eter-
nally present June in January.

"*The Breeding Vegetation.*" Just as Lowell's seasonal imagery oscillates between the two poles of fire and ice, so his plant life is either blighted or menacingly alive. Nothing flowers gradually or gracefully in Lowell's landscape. Yeats's emblematic chestnut tree, that "great-rooted blossomer" whose Romantic sources and analogues Frank Kermode has so beautifully explored,[8] has turned into the "crooked family chestnut" of modern Boston, a "tormented" tree whose "weak-kneed roots" can no longer sustain its growth (*LWC*, 15). Everywhere the poet perceives "the waste / Of the great garden rotten to its root" (*LWC*, 54), a garden of "ailing cedars" (*NO*, 33), and dying elms, "late-lopped, tar-boned, old prunes like stumps of martyrs" (*Nbk*, 124). Even when the trees are in leaf, the leaves are envisioned not as "green" but as "dusty" (*LWC*, 55), "fatigued" (*LS*, 68), "pale," or "nervous" (*Nbk*, 19, 198). Similarly, the grass is either "gray" (*LWC*, 20), "browned" by "dehydration" (*NO*, 46), or "diversified by wounds of sand" (*Nbk*, 60), while the rare flowers in Lowell's world—black-eyed susans, irises, lilacs—are "frizzled" (*LWC*, 17, 55) or "rotting" (*FUD*, 3).

The archetypal garden has become either a barren waste land, as in the above examples, or an oppressive jungle in which creepers catch the poet "by the foot" (*LWC*, 62). In "Terminal Days at Beverly Farms," for example, the imminent death of the poet's father is prefigured by the image of the "scarlet late August sumac, / multiplying like cancer / at their garden's border" (*LS*, 73). In "Man and Wife," the poet, "tamed by Miltown" after a night of fearful insomnia, notes that the "blossoms on our Magnolia ignite / the morning with their murderous five days' white" (*LS*, 87). In the fantasy of the middle-aged poet-lover of *Notebook*, "vermilion leaves" are seen as "clinging like bloodclots to the smitten branch," while blood is "shooting through the fingertips of ivy" and "Grass shooting overnight" (*Nbk*, 31, 35, 28).

The landscape is thus a constant reflection of the poet's own anguish, never an alternative to his malaise as it is for,

say, Williams, Stevens, or Crane. A good example of Lowell's
strategy may be found in "Home after Three Months
Away," in which the speaker wonders whether he can ever
regain the time lost as a result of his recent confinement in a
mental hospital:

> Recuperating, I neither spin nor toil.
> Three stories down below,
> a choreman tends our coffin's length of soil
> and seven horizontal tulips blow.
> Just twelve months ago,
> these flowers were pedigreed
> imported Dutchmen; now no one need
> distinguish them from weed.
> Bushed by the late spring snow,
> they cannot meet
> another year's snowballing enervation.   [*LS*, 84]

In the poet's fractured vision, the garden has become a "coffin's length of soil" and the "seven horizontal tulips," those
"pedigreed / imported Dutchmen" which have turned to
weed, are emblematic of his own precarious cure. He himself
is the "Bushed" tulip, too frail to meet "another year's snow-
balling enervation." Wryly, the poet concludes, "I keep no
rank nor station. / Cured, I am frizzled [an adjective Lowell
regularly applies to flowers], stale and small."

Minerals. Lowell's personae dwell in houses that are shadowed by "the fire-escape's blacker iron, / Isaiah's living coal";
their rooms have aluminum-paint walls (*Nbk*, 260, 22),
metal shaving mirrors (*LS*, 82), and tin wastebaskets (*FUD*,
16). The very sunlight seems "metallic," and the ailing poet
of "Dawn" complains that "Too often my veins are mineral"
(*Nbk*, 112, 92). Like the images of frizzled lilacs and crooked
chestnut trees, the recurrent references to minerals regularly
connote stasis, inflexibility, and death—the "rigor mortis" of
the "braced pig-iron dragons" on the portals of the Hotel de

Ville in the opening poem of *Lord Weary's Castle* (*LWC*, 3). In the early poems, minerals are usually associated with the death of Christianity in the modern world. The Devil has a "golden tongue," and the statue of Christ has been robbed of its spiritual value: "Cold / Snaps the bronze toes and fingers of the Christ / My father fetched from Florence." The Christmas stocking brings no Yuletide joy for it is "full of stones" (*LWC*, 47, 24, 17). More specifically, mineral imagery is associated with the death-in-life of Lowell's Puritan ancestors, whose materialistic greed is typified by their casting of "long lead squids" to catch the innocent "blue-fish" of the Atlantic waters (*LWC*, 9). Arthur Winslow is remembered as an entrepreneur who made a million dollars "Hosing out gold in Colorado's waste," and as hankering for "General Stark's coarse bas relief in bronze," to set upon the granite shaft of his tomb at Dunbarton. Edward Winslow, sheriff and silversmith, made "coin-silver spoons" that rivaled those of the "gaunt Revere" (*LWC*, 21). Two other Winslows, John and Mary, are buried in the shadow of the "golden statehouse dome of Boston." "Frayed cables wreathe their spreading cenotaph. . . . and the laugh / of Death is hacked in sandstone, in their year." Confronted by this landscape of rock, even "the snowmen turn to stone" (*LWC*, 55, 23).

A related but more subtle complex of mineral images is found in the later poem "Sailing Home from Rapallo," whose seasonal imagery has already been discussed. At the Dunbarton family cemetery, "the soil was changing to stone," and the tombs are guarded by a "fence of iron spearhafts." Father Lowell's gravestone is an "unweathered pink-veined slice of marble"; frost has given the names of the dead Winslows and Starks "a diamond edge" (*LS*, 78). The final image of Mrs. Lowell's corpse, "wrapped like *panetone* in Italian tinfoil," which has struck some readers as outrageous,[9] has thus been anticipated all along. Stone, iron, mar-

ble, diamond—these weighty substances yield to the everyday household product: the thin metal sheet of tinfoil (the
pun on "foil" suggests the essential deception of her life), the
image giving us a measure of the triviality, ordinariness, and
pathos of Mrs. Lowell's death.

   "My Last Afternoon with Uncle Devereux Winslow" plays
variations on the same theme.[10] The tension between life
and death is immediately established by the elegy's epitaph:
"1922: the stone porch of my Grandfather's summer house."
The connotations of "stone porch"—lifelessness, the grave,
death—immediately reverse those of "summer house"—
youth, warmth, vitality, life. During the childhood afternoon
recalled by the mature narrator, "Our farmer was cementing
a root-house under the hill," and the little boy who wears
"formal pearl-gray shorts" is depicted as playing with the
piles of black earth and white lime used in this building pro-
ject. The screens of the stone-porch are "black-grained as
drifting coal," and Grandfather's decor is characterized by

> snapshots of his *Liberty Bell* silver mine; . . .
> stogie-brown beams; fools'-gold nuggets;
> octagonal red tiles,
> sweaty with a secret dank, crummy with ant stale.
>
>   [*LS*, 60]

The poplar trees beyond the porch are described as "Diamond-pointed," and even the Scottie puppy is named "Cinder." All these references to mineral imagery look ahead to
the final lines of the poem in which they are explicitly
linked to Uncle Devereux's death:

> My hands were warm, then cool, on the piles
> of earth and lime,
> a black pile and a white pile. . . .
> Come winter,
> Uncle Devereux would blend to the one color.
>
>   [*LS*, 64; spaced dots, Lowell's]

In the later poetry, Lowell uses fewer references to stone, gold, or diamonds; the marble gravestones and bronze monuments give way to the "dead metal" of industry. The poet moves uneasily about this landscape of "car keys and razor blades," "stapled pasture wire" (*FUD*, 36, 37, 65), and "lacework groins as tall as twenty trees" (*Nbk*, 35). Behind a "barbed and galvanized fence," "yellow dinosaur steamshovels" ominously prepare for the transformation of Boston Common into an "underworld garage" and a "girdle of orange, Puritan-pumpkin colored girders / braces the tingling Statehouse, / shaking over the excavations" (*FUD*, 70–71). The "Mosler Safe" in a storefront window on Boylston Street has become our new Rock of Ages. Taken in isolation, this image in "For the Union Dead" is a bitterly ironic reference to the fate of the Church in the modern world. But since rock is always a death image in Lowell's poetry, there is a further irony in the passage: the Mosler Safe has "survived the blast" because in fact it has no life to lose; its safety is that of death.

"The Bestiary-Garden By My Cell." In the Lowell country, the tiger has vanished from the forests of the night leaving behind the "tiger kitten, *Oranges*," who cartwheels about "in a ball of snarls" (*LS*, 54). The Biblical serpent—a conventional symbol used in the early poetry—soon gives way to such lesser reptiles as the turtle; in the same way, the whale and lion of the early poems are replaced by the "cowed, compliant fish" of "For the Union Dead" (*FUD*, 70) and the imaginary "broken-hearted lions" who lick Santayana's hand in the "worn arena" of his magnifying glass (*LS*, 52). Again, the Christian eagle and dove, briefly glimpsed in *Lord Weary's Castle*, give way to barnyard fowl: in *Life Studies*, Santayana is nursed by "geese-girl sisters"; the poet and his friend Delmore Schwartz have a stuffed duck as their trophy and fight "the chicken-hearted shadows of the

world"; and the feverish little daughter of the poet "floun-
ders in her chicken-colored sleeping bag" (51, 53, 79).

When wild animals and exotic birds do appear in the later
poems, they are always placed in ironic contexts. Thus Ford
Madox Ford, middle-aged, obese, and short-winded, is pictured as a "mammoth mumbler," an "unforgetting ele-
phant"; the efficient baby nurse is "a lioness who ruled the
roost"; the poet's neurasthenic spinster Aunt Sarah rises
"like the phoenix / from her bed of troublesome snacks and
Tauchnitz classics"; the poet himself sees his boyhood image
in the mirror as that of a "stuffed toucan / with a bibulous,
multicolored beak" (*LS*, 50, 83, 61). The poet of *Notebook,*
lusting after a certain girl in Mexico, is "like a bull with a
ring in its nose"; or again, his beloved is pictured as a heron
with a warped neck, "a broken pick" (103, 84).

Ironic references to the nobler animals and birds thus
function to point up the pettiness of mankind. Not surprisingly, therefore, the predominant animal images in Lowell's
poetry are those of noxious insects, spiders, amphibians, and
rodents burrowing in the earth. From the mouse who
"Cracks walnuts by the headstones of the dead" (*LWC,* 57)
to the "live muskrat," obsessively "muddying the moonlight"
in the second "Charles River" sonnet (*Nbk,* 67), Lowell's
poems have been full of references to mice, cats, moles, chip-
munks, otters, worms, caterpillars, gnats, flies, spiders, bats,
locusts, parrots, and geese as images of pettiness, blindness,
ugliness, disease, and death.

In this respect, Lowell's bestiary has remained essentially
unchanged since *Lord Weary's Castle,* but increasingly the
poet reads his own sense of futility into the activities of the
insect and animal world. In "Fall 1961," for example, the
speaker, exhausted by the "chafe and jar / of nuclear war,"
exclaims, "I swim like a minnow / behind my studio window," and concludes that "We are like a lot of wild / spiders
crying together, / but without tears" (*FUD,* 11). Similarly,

the speaker of "Dunbarton" suddenly sees himself as a "young newt, / neurasthenic, scarlet / and wild in the wild coffee-colored water" (*LS*, 66).

The poet's attempts at finding love are often placed in the ironic perspective of insect images: he and his beloved are "quivering and fierce . . . simmering like wasps / in our tent of books!" or like "Two walking cobwebs, almost bodiless" (*FUD*, 6, 67), or "two fray-winged dragonflies, / clinging to a thistle" (*Nbk*, 28). The middle-aged poet, longing for love, realizes he is a "fagged insect" who "splinters to rejoin / the infinite"; he sees himself reflected in "the ant's cool, amber, hyperthyroid eye" (*Nbk*, 66, 27).

Distasteful as these insects and animals are to the poet, he cannot kill them without compunction. Thus, in "The Neoclassical Urn," the speaker is haunted by the bitter memory of a childhood pastime: killing turtles and dropping them "splashing in our garden urn, / like money in the bank." In his imagination, he now identifies with the dead turtles ("I rub my skull, / that turtle shell"), breathing "their dying smell" and watching "their crippled last survivors pass, / and hobble humpbacked through the grizzled grass" (*FUD*, 47–48). In the end, then, the positions of man and turtle are reversed: it is the poet who is trapped in the urn, while the turtles have inherited the earth. A similar incident is recorded in one of the first sonnets of *Notebook:* the speaker is obsessed by a "repeating fly, blueblack, thumbthick—so gross, / It seems apocalyptic in our house" (21). Scathingly, he compares it to a "plane / gunning potato bugs or Arabs on the screen," and nonchalantly kills it. But as he sweeps the dead fly under the carpet, it seems to be "wrinkling to fulfillment." The killing of the fly has accomplished nothing because the insects and rodents of Lowell's world are, after all, no more than projections of his own mental landscape. A rare exception is the mother skunk of "Skunk Hour," whose energy ("moonstruck eyes' red fire") and vital commitment to her young remind the poet that an outside world, more positive and alive than his fractured sense of it, does exist.

The Social and Psychological Milieu

> I hear
> my ill-spirit sob in each blood cell.
> "Skunk Hour"

If Lowell's imaginative landscape were limited to the nature imagery considered in the preceding section, it would not be particularly distinctive. The pathetic fallacy has, after all, been with us for a long time, and from Eliot on, it has been standard poetic practice to paint gloomy pictures of the "dead land," the "withered stumps of time," man as a doomed insect, and so on. But when Lowell's nature imagery is viewed in the context of his treatment of man's social and psychological environment, the originality of his poetry becomes much more apparent. Lowell is essentially a humanist poet, and the external world does not become really interesting to him unless he can explore its relationship to the human mind. Not the physical setting itself, but the actual *feel* of living in it—this is the theme to which I now turn.

Noise. In Lowell's unreal city, sound itself has become man's enemy. Everywhere one meets harsh, grating, and sometimes terrifying noises. The inhabitants of this world never speak to each other in normal voices: they scream, screech, wail, groan, and cry. The juke box "booms" (*LWC,* 6), "officer-professors" crash into Santayana's hospital room (*LS,* 51), and the snowplow groans as it charges uphill (*FUD,* 6). The poet's auditory nerve is so raw that even the sound of high heels pounding the city pavement becomes unbearable: "Manhattan is pierced by the stiletto heel." When an ordinary sheet of onion skin typewriter paper was pulled from its pack, the poet recalls, it "seemed to scream" (*Nbk,* 126, 43).

Noise is often associated with the violence of war, especially in the early poetry. The attack of the Indian King Philip is seen as taking place in a "wailing valley," and his "death-dance" is accompanied by a "scream / Whose echo girdled this imperfect globe" (*LWC*, 54, 27). In "The Quaker Graveyard in Nantucket," violent noise, whether referring to the sea battles of World War II or to the whale hunt in *Moby Dick,* is almost monotonously pervasive: "yawing S-boats splash / The bellbuoy, with ballooning spinnakers, / As the entangled screeching mainsheet clears / The blocks"; "Guns . . . blast the eelgrass"; "The bones cry for the blood of the white whale"; "the winds' wings . . . scream," and "thunder shakes the white surf" (*LWC,* 9, 10, 12).

But the scream of modern man persists in peacetime as well as in war. The new metropolis inevitably breeds noise: "New York / drills through my nerves," as the poet puts it in "Middle Age" (*FUD,* 7). Standing in the cemetery behind King's Chapel in Boston, the poet sadly thinks that even in the graveyard there is no silence: "A green train grinds along its buried tracks / And screeches" (*LWC,* 56). On another train, "Crossing the Alps," the stewards "go / forward on tiptoe banging on their gongs" (*LS,* 3), while the wheels make a "querulous hush-hush" sound. The voice of the Third Avenue El becomes a symbol of the futility and despair the poet feels in "Inauguration Day: January 1953":

> The subways drummed the vaults. I heard
> the El's green girders charge on Third,
> Manhattan's truss of adamant,
> that groaned in ermine.   [*LS,* 7]

In such a setting, music has a tinny or off sound. The poet of *Life Studies* recalls how his spinster Aunt Sarah "thundered on the keyboard of her dummy piano." His "rattley little country gramophone" makes a "racking" sound, while his car radio "bleats, / 'Love, O careless Love' " (*LS,* 61, 68,

90). Even radiators make unpleasant music. In his "dull and alien room," the poet, unable to sleep, watches the "white pipes, / ramrods of steam," and notes, "I hear / the lonely metal breathe / and gurgle like the sick" (*FUD*, 31–32). In a similar image in *Notebook,* the "overworked central heating bangs the frame, / as a milkhorse in childhood, would crash the morning milkcan" (*Nbk,* 81). The rasping of the "dangling telephone receiver" (*LWC*, 43), the grunting of the "yellow dinosaur steamshovels" (*FUD*, 70), a colleague's typing that sounds like a "popping bonfire," the cement mixer's "choir of locusts" (*Nbk,* 106, 209)—these are the sounds, Lowell implies, that we live with every day—sounds we somehow never get used to no matter how constant they are.

But sound does not just bombard us from outside; it also comes from within. "The Scream," based on an Elizabeth Bishop short story, depicts a girl's memory of her mother's gradually deteriorating mental condition. She recalls the fatal day when her mother was taken to the asylum: "she gave the scream, / not even loud at first" and "went away" (*FUD,* 9). Although the girl tries to forget the auditory image, she knows that she will remember that scream for the rest of her life. Similar moments occur in other poems. In "Mary Winslow," the poet recalls the "hideous baby-squawks and yells" of his dying relative; in "The Death of the Sheriff," the protagonist "howled for weeks" after he had been committed to a mental hospital; only his death brought quiet (*LWC,* 25, 65).

Many of Lowell's personae are characterized by their vocal quality. His mother in her middle years retained a voice that was "still electric / with a hysterical, unmarried panic." Father Lowell, less sophisticated than his wife, "boomed in his bathtub, / 'Anchors aweigh.' " Lowell's wife is pictured as a young girl at a Greenwich Village party: "the shrill verve / of your invective scorched the traditional South," whereas "twelve years later," "your old-fashioned tirade— / loving, rapid, merciless— / breaks like the Atlantic Ocean on my head" (*LS*, 70, 71, 87).

Just like the idolatrous crowds at St. Peter's who "screamed *Papa*" (*LS*, 4), the birds and animals described in the preceding section of this chapter participate in the universal cry. We have already noted the image of the "wild / spiders crying together" (*FUD*, 11). The canaries of "In the Cage," Lowell's first prison poem, "beat their bars and scream." In "At the Indian Killer's Grave," the gulls "Scream from the squelching wharf-piles" (*LWC*, 53, 56), announcing that Judgment Day is coming. In *Notebook*, seagulls similarly have an "exaggerated outcry" and utter "groans like straining rope" (*Nbk*, 22, 26). The "false fin de siecle decorum" of modern Buenos Aires is symbolized by the "bulky, beefy breathing of the herds" which disturbs the poet's sleep even though he cannot actually hear it in his hotel room (*FUD*, 60). Even in the lonely countryside, the self is unprotected from noise: an "unknown nightbird" voices his "after curfew / boom" or a fly "whams back and forth" (*Nbk*, 26, 21).

The self in Lowell's poetry is hypersensitive to noise because his own music is so dangerous. "Sometimes," he says in the sonnet "In Sickness," "my mind is a rocked and dangerous bell, / I climb the spiral steps to my own music" (*Nbk*, 57). Sounds are thus magnified in the poet's private bell jar, whose spiral staircase, unlike Yeats's winding stair, leads absolutely nowhere. Thus the mental world and the external world become mirror images: whether the sounds are real or imaginary no longer matters.

Motion. In the Lowell country, objects never touch gently; there is always a head-on collision. The very air, for example, is always in churning, violent, chaotic motion: the "chemical air" that "sweeps in from New Jersey" overwhelms the "unforgivable landscape" (*FUD*, 10). One of the central images of "The Quaker Graveyard in Nantucket" is the destructive wind, whose "wings beat upon the stones" and whose "claws rush / At the sea's throat and wring it in the slush" (*LWC*, 9). Throughout *Lord Weary's Castle*, this wind image recurs: "The March-winds lift and cry", "storm-clouds shelter Christmas", the blizzard "mounts in squalls", and the gate of the old palace is "wind-torn" (15, 17, 3). In a much later poem, "Soft Wood," the image of the wind "blasting an all-white wall whiter" and "smashing without direction" mirrors the poet's desolation in the face of his cousin's recent death. In one of the *Notebook* sonnets, "These Winds," the poet, half-listening to his daughter playing the piano downstairs, absently looks out of his study window:

> I see these winds, these are the tops of trees,
> these are no heavier than green alder bushes:
> touched by a light wind, they begin to mingle
> and race for instability—too well placed
> to last out a day in the brush, these are the winds.

As the meditation continues, "these winds" are seen as the force that cancels out the much less certain "wind of inspiration"; they spell death not only to the alder bushes but also to the poet contemplating the frightening passage of time that has elapsed since his daughter, now at the piano, was born. The wind, as the speaker puts it in the last line, is the "unreliable touch of the all" (*Nbk*, 238).

Not only wind but motion in general is regarded as a destructive force. In *Lord Weary's Castle*, guns "split up timber / And nick the slate roofs"; the "jack-hammer jabs into the ocean"; the "treadmill night / Churns up Long Island Sound" (3, 5, 6). Wandering through post-World War II Europe with its rubble heaps, the poet hears "the earth's reverberations" (*LWC*, 68). In "For the Union Dead," the excavation of the "underworld garage" underneath the Boston

Common is seen in his imagination as an "earthquake" (*FUD*, 71). Even in the Maine sonnets of *Notebook*, the mood is not one of tranquillity: the "bite" of the chainsaw, the "mangle and mash" of the power mower, and the "Shake of the electric fan about our village" destroy the narrator's peace (21, 28, 27).

Persons, animals, plants, or inanimate objects move about the landscape with speed, abrupt change of position, and violent gesture. The "Paris Pullman," for example, does not glide quietly through the night; it seems to "lunge / mooning across the fallow Alpine snow" (*LS*, 3). Similarly, the poet's grandparents do not drive to town on Fridays; they go "champing for their ritual Friday spin" (*LS*, 68). The spiders of Lowell's first Jonathan Edwards poem meet their death "Urgently beating East to sunrise and the sea" (*LWC*, 58). At mealtime, the inmates of a Munich mental hospital "shoot / like starlight through their air-conditioned bowl"; in another mental hospital, "Bobbie," the anachronistic Harvard alumnus, "swashbuckles about in his birthday suit / and horses at chairs." Even the defunct "summer millionaire" of "Skunk Hour" is remembered by the poet as a figure that "seemed to leap from an L. L. Bean / Catalogue" (*LS*, 8, 82, 89).

Outer violence is matched by inner turmoil; physiologically, man is regarded as a "stunned machine" (*LWC*, 5), furiously charging and discharging energy. In "Colloquy in Black Rock," the poet, submitting to the "nigger-brass percussions" of his heart beat, is "rattled screw and footloose" (*LWC*, 5). Fighting insomnia in "Myopia: A Night," his "five senses clenched / their teeth." Looking down on Manhattan from his skyscraper window, he is aware of his breath "sawing and pumping to the terminal" (*FUD*, 32, 65). Walking with a "short-skirted girl" along the Charles River, he feels the "thumping and pumping of overfevered zeal"; on a rendezvous with another girl, he senses that "our clasped il-

licit hands / pulse, stop the bloodstream as if it hit rock"
(*Nbk,* 66, 53).

In Lowell's poetic universe, even the "circular moon" no
longer rises slowly in the heavens; it "saw-wheels up the
oak-grove" (*Nbk,* 246). The graceful rhythms of ordered existence have been lost; there is no calm, stability, or peace.
Interestingly, the vocabulary of contemporary drug culture
—"shoot," "speed," "trip," "blew it," "strung out"—is very
much the vocabulary used to describe the wind-torn, electri-
cally charged, pumping, reverberating landscape of Lowell's
poems.

"Industry's Dogged, Clogged Pollution." Lowell's Inferno,
unlike the empty desert of Rimbaud's "Saison en Enfer," is a
noisy land of plenty where objects are wastefully discarded
or mistreated so that they rust, break, decay, mildew, or
drown in grease. The poet's imagination is haunted by the
spectre of "the man / scavenging filth in the back alley trash
cans"; he cannot forget the "red fox stain" that seems to
cover, not only "Blue Hill," but the entire universe (*LS,*
85, 89).

Unlike Wordsworth's early morning Thames, a river that
"glideth at his own sweet will," or Eliot's "strong brown
God," or Crane's sensually female Mississippi, which gracefully meets the Gulf and "hosannas silently below," Lowell's
Hudson is a stagnant body of water, sitting uneasily between
"ledges of suburban factories" and the "chains of condemned
freight trains / from thirty states" (*FUD,* 10). Similarly,
Lowell's ocean is not the sea of life; it is "fouled with the
blue sailors" who have drowned in it and glutted with "bilge
and backwash"; in Salem harbor, "sewage sickens the rebel-
lious seas" (*LWC,* 14, 10, 26). And the transition from ocean
to land brings no relief: the "hermit / heiress" of Nautilus
Island makes a feeble attempt to change things by buying up
"all / the eyesores facing her shore," but lethargically "lets

them fall" (*LS*, 89). Thus, even in his favorite Maine resort, the poet notes that "The shore is pebbled with eroding brick, / seaweed in grizzled furrows. . . . sticks of dead rotten wood in drifts" (*Nbk*, 28).

Moving inland, past the "rotten lake" (*LWC*, 20) and the "humus-sallowed pool," the poet traverses mud-flats where "watermelons gutted to the crust" are strewn about, crosses "seedy fields" (62, 5, 63), and walks along sidewalks "smeared with dogmess," past "palisades of garbage cans" (*Dolphin*, 8). Both the "muck" on the "chewed-up streets" of New York (*FUD*, 7), and the "dry road dust" which "rises to whiten / the fatigued elm leaves" (*LS*, 68) whenever a car speeds by, seem to penetrate the poet's very being: "the dust / Is on this skipping heart that shakes my house" (*LWC*, 5).

The very houses reflect the same general decay. A cannon, emblematic of the Civil War, is "Rusting before the blackened Statehouse" in Boston, and "rusty mire" covers the Hotel de Ville in the heart of the Rhineland (*LWC*, 17, 3). The silhouette of the grimy concrete dome of M. I. T. reminds the poet of Nero's Rome: its architecture comes to symbolize "the blood of the spirit lost in veins of brickdust" (*Nbk*, 69). From the "roof of the West Street Jail," the Hudson River is visible "through sooty clothesline entanglements / and bleaching khaki tenements" (*LS*, 86). And here is the Boston skyscape seen from the poet's window:

> Sloping, torn tarpaper on a wet roof,
> on several roofs; here and there a stray nail,
> background of wrecked gingerbread Gothic . . .
>
> [*Nbk*, 46]

Behind the facades of these shaky houses, there is the same process of decay and decomposition. In "Night Sweat," the feverish poet regards his "work-table, litter, books and standing lamp, / plain things, my stalled equipment," and shudders as he feels the "creeping damp / float over my pajamas' wilted white" (*FUD*, 68). In his Maine cottage, "moldy splinters fall / in sawdust from the aluminum-paint wall, / once loud and fresh, now aged to weathered wood" (*Nbk,* 22). Termites are "digging in the underpinning" (*FUD*, 65), and the "spineless vermin slink stinking from the woodwork" (*Nbk 67,* 46). Even in "Buttercups," a poem ostensibly about happy childhood afternoons in the attic, the speaker especially remembers the "huge cobwebbed print of Waterloo, / with a cracked smile across the glass" (*LWC,* 18).

Unlike Wallace Stevens' "Man on the Dump," who "sits and beats an old tin can, lard pail," contemplating the trash around him without feeling directly responsible for its presence, Lowell's speaker claims no such philosophical detachment. Crossing the lawn one summer evening after a family lobster dinner, he becomes aware of

> the simmer
> of the moon's mildew on the same pile of shells,
> fruits of the banquet . . . boiled a brittle lobster-
> shell-red, the hollow foreclaw, cracked, sucked dry,
> flung on the ash-heap of a soggy carton—
> two burnt-out, pinhead, black and popping eyes.
> [*Nbk,* 24–25; spaced dots, Lowell's]

The "burnt-out . . . popping eyes" of the devoured lobster are a grotesque reminder of man's careless treatment of his environment. As the poet sardonically declares earlier in the sonnet, "The fires men build live after them."

The "Underworld Garage." The shrill sounds, the violent movements, the polluted air and trash heaps that characterize our civilization—all these are embodied in one of Lowell's most obsessive images—the automobile. I can think of no other poet who has so lovingly and carefully studied the world of fenders (*LWC,* 4), car radios (*LS,* 90), tires, hoods, and brakes (*Nbk,* 93, 44, 27) as has Lowell. The automobile, as he presents it, stands at the very center of our existence, controlling our movements rather than vice-versa. In "Skunk Hour," for example, the poet's night ride hardly seems a matter of conscious volition, for the car itself makes the decisions ("One dark night / my Tudor Ford climbed the hill's skull"), while the "love-cars" for which the speaker watches seem to have an eerie life of their own: "Lights turned down, / they lay together, hull to hull" (*LS*, 90). When Grandpa used to drive to Dunbarton, the poet recalls in another autobiographical poem, "Freed from Karl [his chauffeur] and chuckling over the gas he was saving, / he let his motor roller-coaster / out of control down each hill" (*LS*, 65).

Thus man has invented a new monster, more powerful and sinister than those he has tamed; *out of control,* it roller-coasters down the hills of the twentieth-century continent. This monster frightens the oxen who "blunder hugely up St. Peter's Hill" to visit the holy manger; they "drool and start / In wonder at the fenders of a car" (*LWC,* 4). The incestuous heroine of "Her Dead Brother" is terrified as her husband's Packard "crunches up the drive" (*MK*, 31). In "For the Union Dead," the "dark, downward, and vegetating kingdom / of the fish and reptile" has been replaced by the "savage servility" of "giant finned cars" that "nose forward like fish" (*FUD*, 72). Even in an isolated little Mexican village, "buses eat up the sidewalk" (*Nbk,* 104). The very seasons, Lowell notes in one of the *Dolphin* sonnets, "race engines in America" (4).

Ironically enough, man tries with all his might to make friends with the automobile, to domesticate this steel and chrome monster as if it were a new pony to be bred. No wonder that Grandpa Winslow's Pierce Arrow "clears its throat in a horse stall" (*LS*, 68). In "91 Revere Street" and its companion poems, the stages of decline in Commander Lowell's civilian career are comically defined by the series of cars he buys: "Almost immediately . . . he sold his ascetic, stove-black Hudson and bought a plump brown Buick; later the Buick was exchanged for a high-toned, as good-as-new Packard with a custom-designed royal blue and mahogany body. Without drama, his earnings more or less decreased from year to year" (LS, 15–16).

The adjectives in this passage are noteworthy: most are applicable to persons or animals rather than to machines: *ascetic, plump, brown, high-toned*. The same kind of animism is found in a later passage: "He had just broken in a new car. Like a chauffeur, he watched this car, a Hudson, with an informed vigilance, always giving its engine hair-trigger little tinkerings of adjustment or friendship, always fearful lest the black body, unbeautiful as his boiled shirts, should lose its outline and gloss. He drove with flawless, almost instrumental monotony" (LS, 23). Father Lowell thus breaks in his car as if it were a thoroughbred; he guards its "black body" with "informed vigilance" and trembles for its safety as if it were his own child. Shortly before his death, he makes friends with still another car:

> Father had had two coronaries.
> He still treasured underhand economies,
> but his best friend was his little black *Chevie,*
> garaged like a sacrificial steer
> with gilded hooves,
> yet sensationally sober,
> and with less side than an old dancing pump.   [LS, 74]

Here the owner wholly identifies with his automobile, a gorgeous steer with gilded hooves, willing to be led to sacrifice, a "sober" traveller, a sleek, glossy black creature more graceful than a dancing pump.

Once man has automobiles rather than horses in his stable, his dependency becomes complete, and the silence of parked cars is even more oppressive than the screech of their engines or the carbon monoxide that escapes from their exhausts. In "Alba," the poet, standing at his apartment-house window, faces the anxiety of a new dawn: "thirty stories seem hundreds, / with miniature-view windows that gleam like cells." Scanning the deserted early-morning streets of New York, he concludes that there is "Nothing more established, pure and lonely, / than the early Sunday morning in New York— / the sun on high burning, and most cars dead" (*Nbk*, 57). Similarly, in "Blizzard at Cambridge," the absence of the customary traffic makes him nervous: "everything mechanical stopped dead: / taxis thumbs-down on fares, tires burning the ice" (*Nbk*, 93).

In the final analysis, the modern sensibility cannot do with cars and cannot do without them. Rationally, Lowell's speaker despises these mechanical monsters, and yet he senses their terrible power to make one a part of the "going generation":

> it's the same for me
> at fifty as at thirteen, my childish thirst
> to be the grown-up in his open car and girl. . . .
> She straddles the hood and snuffs the dust of twilight:
> "I want to live," she screams, "where I can see."
> [*Nbk*, 44; spaced dots, Lowell's]

Prison. Surveying the Lowell landscape, one notices that it seems to be parceled out and divided up into small lots, and everywhere there are bars, fences, walls, nets, and nooses. One is either outside the barrier, trying to get in or inside trying to get out. In "The Indian Killer's Grave," for example, the man at the subway turnstile is described as the "doorman" who "barricades you in and out" (*LWC*, 57). For Lowell, as for Eliot, the individual is imprisoned behind the walls of his own ego: Ugolino's famous speech in *The Waste Land:* "I have heard the key / Turn in the door once and turn once only / We think of the key, each in his prison" is echoed by Lowell's recurrent prison images although Lowell does not, like Eliot, blame modern man's isolation, restriction, and sense of confinement on his removal from Christ, but rather stresses man's loss of ethical values as well as the failure of society as a whole organism.

A number of poems are explicitly about prisons or famous prisoners: for example, the sonnets on Abelard, Joinville, or Che Guevara (*Nbk*, 189, 76, 53). "In the Cage," which first appeared in *Lord Weary's Castle* and is reprinted in *Notebook*, had its origins in Lowell's own prison term as a conscientious objector in World War II:

> The lifers file into the hall,
> According to their houses—twos
> Of laundered denim. On the wall
> A colored fairy tinkles blues
> And titters by the balustrade;
> Canaries beat their bars and scream.   [*LWC*, 53] [11]

In this hallucinatory picture of prison life, everything merges: the jailbirds and the canary birds, the titter of the "colored fairy" and the canary's "scream," the balustrade and the prison bars. A less violent, more detached view of the same scene is found in "Memories of West Street and Lepke":

> Given a year,
> I walked on the roof of the West Street Jail, a short
> enclosure like my school soccer court,
> and saw the Hudson River once a day
> through sooty clothesline entanglements
> and bleaching khaki tenements.   [*LS*, 85–86]

Here the comparison of jail roof and soccer court cuts both ways: perhaps the jail roof is a fairly benign place since it resembles a school soccer court; on the other hand, Lowell implies that a school soccer court is also a kind of prison. Even the Hudson River cannot flow freely; it is hemmed in by walls ("bleaching khaki tenements") and roped off by "sooty clothesline entanglements."

"No fence stands up between us and our object," the poet

says sardonically in one of the "Those Older" sonnets, as he surveys a pitiful little country cemetery in an exposed and open field, surrounded by "dead timber" that is "bulldozed rootless" (*Nbk,* 124). There seems to be little choice between such unfenced "desert places" and the more usual condition in which fences do stand up "between us and our object." "When we were children," the speaker of "Buttercups" recalls, "We were shut / In gardens" (*LWC,* 18), thus reversing the normal connotations of the garden. In the Dunbarton family cemetery, the dead are wholly shut in: "A fence of iron spear-hafts / black-bordered its mostly Colonial grave slates" (*LS,* 77). Seen from the outside, the apartment building on Central Park West in which the poet lives is nothing but a prison, with its "two water tanks, tanned shingle, corsetted / by stapled pasture wire" (*FUD,* 65). In "For the Union Dead," both the childhood scene in the aquarium and the adult scene at Colonel Shaw's monument feature fenced places. The child standing outside the fish tank, trying to penetrate the glass and "burst the bubbles / drifting from the noses of the cowed, compliant fish," is juxtaposed to the disenchanted adult, standing outside a more sinister enclosure:

> One morning last March
> I pressed against the new barbed and galvanized
>
> fence on the Boston Common. Behind their cage,
> yellow dinosaur steamshovels were grunting
> as they cropped up tons of mush and grass
> to gouge their underworld garage.   [*FUD,* 70]

Although it is the "dinosaur steamshovels" that are behind the cage, the speaker's anxiety suggests that the real cage is his own; it exists this side of the barbed-wire fence. Similarly, Randall Jarrell's movements, during the harrowing night drive which culminated in suicide, remind the poet of a "caged squirrel on its wheel" (*Nbk,* 50). Because the poet cannot forget his own sense of confinement, he sees animals as being trapped as well. Up in a little Maine lobster town, the "fish for bait" are "trapped" inside "the little matchstick / mazes of a weir." At his country house, a muskrat is similarly trapped in a packing crate which "it furiously slashed to matchwood to escape" (*FUD*, 3, 16).

On a sleepless night, the poet sees his "dull and alien room" as a "cell of learning" (*FUD*, 31), and indeed rooms are often referred to as cells in Lowell's poetry. The "officer-professors of philosophy" come crashing through the "cell" (in reality, the small hospital room at the Convent of Santo Stefano) of George Santayana (*LS*, 51). The buildings of New York have "miniature view-windows that gleam like cells" (*Nbk*, 57). Or again, referring to himself and his wife in their twentieth-floor apartment, Lowell puns on the word *cell:* "bed to bed, / we two, one cell here, lie / gazing into the ether's crystal ball, / sky and a sky, and sky, and sky, till death" (*FUD*, 65).

Boxes, tin cans, and nets regularly act as prisons. In "New Year's Day," after the kitten has "heaved its hindlegs, as if fouled, and died," the poet remembers that "We bent it in a Christmas box" (*LWC*, 7). In "Dunbarton," little Bob Lowell idly pokes some newts with his grandfather's cane:

> In a tobacco tin after capture, the umber yellow mature
> newts
> lost their leopard spots,
> lay grounded as numb
> as scrolls of candied grapefruit peel.   [*LS*, 66]

Suddenly the poet sees himself as a "young newt, / neurasthenic, scarlet." His world is also a tobacco tin just as the state becomes, in his imagination, "a diver under a glass bell" (*FUD*, 11). Even when making love, Lowell's speaker feels ultimately trapped. Trying to define the moment of union, he says, "we are two species, even from the inside— / a net trapped in the arms of another net" (*Nbk*, 45).

Hospital. From the early "Death from Cancer," in which the poet moralizes on his Grandfather Winslow's "wrestling with the crab" (*LWC*, 19), to the recent "Half a Century Gone" (*Nbk*, 258), in which the speaker says of death: "I feel the woven cycles of His pain, / reticulations of His spawning cells / the intimations of my family cancer," Lowell's human beings are depicted as essentially diseased, whether the illness is physical or mental, whether the diagnosis is cerebral hemorrhage, coronary thrombosis (*LS*, 8, 73), or a mere case of "molar drain" (*Nbk*, 82). In the words of Lowell's Jonathan Edwards, "You play against a sickness past your cure" (*LWC*, 58).

Before we discuss Lowell's disease images, it might be helpful to define the poet's attitude toward the human body in general. Prufrock, we recall, was haunted by "arms that are braceleted and white and bare / but in the lamplight downed with light brown hair." Yeats's favorite organ of the body is the heart, while Hart Crane refers repeatedly to the eye as the instrument of vision. But Lowell cares less for the heart or the eye than for those outer extremities, the hands and feet. The Lowell universe is mysteriously peopled by disembodied fingers and toes, palms and heels, reaching out toward something or someone. When the "I" weeps, tears do not bathe his cheeks as one might expect—they "smut my fingers" (*LS*, 69).

In the earlier poetry, the hand is given the conventional connotations of authority, possessiveness, and control. "What are we in the hands of the great God?" Jonathan Edwards asks (*LWC*, 58), and Marie de Medici exults that her son Louis XIII's "dimpled fingers clutch Versailles" (*LS*, 6). But the larger significance of hands in Lowell's poetry is that of contact and communication—the touch that relates one person to another. Conversely, when hands do not touch, there is alienation, isolation, or withdrawal into the self.

In "Man and Wife," for example, the speaker gratefully

acknowledges that his wife has helped him to survive one more anxiety attack:

> All night I've held your hand
> as if you had
> a fourth time faced the kingdom of the mad
> its hackneyed speech, its homicidal eye—
> and dragged me home alive.   [*LS*, 87]

In the harsh light of day, however, she turns her back on the poet, hugging not him but her pillow. Similarly, in "Child's Song," the "little muddler" tries to derive comfort from touching a loved one: "Sometimes I touch your hand / across my cot, / and our fingers knot." But then he sadly realizes that "there's no hand / to take me home" (*FUD*, 22).

In "For the Union Dead," the hand measures the gulf between past and present. During the poet's childhood, the aquarium was a magical place: "my hand tingled / to burst the bubbles / drifting from the noses of the cowed, compliant fish." But now the formerly "airy tanks" are dry and so "My hand draws back" (*FUD*, 70). The withdrawing hand measures the poet's retreat into himself. Similarly, the speaker of "The Flaw" nostalgically remembers a former love affair as a time when "Your fingertips . . . touched my fingertips" (*FUD*, 67).

Like the hand, the foot is an image expressing contact with the outside world, although in this case, the contact is less a matter of personal communication than of sheer physical survival in an alien environment. Lowell's characters move about on tiptoe because they cannot quite reach the earth below their feet. Thus the stewards on the Paris Pullman of "Beyond the Alps" "go / forward on tiptoe banging on their gongs," and Father Lowell observes a nightly ritual of tiptoeing down the stairs to chain the front door. After his death, his "town-house furniture / had an on tiptoe air / of waiting for the mover / on the heels of the undertaker" (*LS*,

3, 79, 76). Even the old-fashioned highboy, one of Father's heirlooms, is seen as "quaking to its toes" when father and son have one of their periodic fights (*LWC*, 29). Flying south to Brazil, the poet has the terrible sense of being hurled through outer space to his death:

> I have lost my foothold on the map,
> now falling, falling, bent, intense, my feet
> breaking my clap of thunder on the street.   [*FUD*, 62]

The only creatures, it seems, whose feet do make firm contact with the earth are not people at all but skunks: "They march on their soles up Main Street" (*LS*, 90).

The foot that no longer performs its function is a frequent symptom of impending death. Ford Madox Ford's indigent last days in New York are recalled in the lines: "the bales of your left-over novels buy / less than a bandage for your gouty foot." After a night of drunken self-flagellation, Lowell and Delmore Schwartz remove the web-foot from a stuffed duck —Schwartz's hunting trophy—and stick it into "a quart of gin we'd killed" (*LS*, 50, 54). And Ezra Pound, in dialogue with Lowell, says he has come to realize that it has been his fate " 'To begin with a swelled head and end with swelled feet' " (*Nbk*, 120).

Just as the foot can no longer play its proper role, so the eye cannot see properly. All too often, "Some mote, some eye-flaw, wobbles in the heat" (*FUD*, 66) and clouds the poet's vision. He is haunted by bulging eye-balls, "hollow sockets" (*MK*, 54, 38), or eyes flushed by the "Wine of idleness" (*Imit*, 91). The famous poem "Eye and Tooth" in *For the Union Dead* has as its germ the very ordinary experience of getting something in one's eye. As Irvin Ehrenpreis has observed, the poem depends on a "brilliant use of the *eye-I* pun. . . . The dominating metaphor is, so to speak, 'I've got something in my I and can't get it out.' " [12] Flinching from the pain ("My whole eye was sunset red, / the old cut cornea

throbbed"), the poet retraces similar moments in the past
when the eye was assaulted, not by a physical mote but by
the vision of something ugly or disquieting, the implication
being that all the earlier incidents foreshadowed the actual
physical injury to the eye that he has just received: "Young,
my eyes began to fail." The poem ends on an ironic note:
the only solution to his dilemma, the speaker senses, is not
to take his "I" too seriously; everyone, including the patient
himself, is bored with his suffering:

> Nothing! No oil
> for the eye, nothing to pour
> on those waters or flames.
> I am tired. Everyone's tired of my turmoil.   [*FUD,* 19]

Lowell frequently dwells on the poignant gap between the
outer appearance of health and the inner reality of disease.
Uncle Devereux Winslow, for example, strikes young Bob
Lowell as a marvelously "animated" and "hierarchical"
figure in his "blue coat and white trousers" which "grew
sharper and straighter," but in fact he is "dying of the incurable Hodgkin's disease." Similarly, Father Lowell meets his
"abrupt and unprotesting" death on a morning of "anxious,
repetitive smiling" when he looks "bronzed, breezy" and "vi-
tally trim" (*LS,* 64, 73–74). In "Waking in the Blue," Stanley, one of the poet's fellow mental patients at McLean's in
Boston, is "still hoarding the build of a boy in his twenties"
although the ex-football player is now "sunk in his sixties."
The poet himself, healthy and well-fed, is the "Cock of the
walk" in this mental hospital; he struts up to the "metal
shaving mirrors" with a self-confidence which rapidly evaporates as he sees "the shaky future grow familiar / in the
pinched, indigenous faces" of his companions, and realizes
that "each of us holds a locked razor" (*LS,* 81, 82). The
phrase "We are all old-timers" in the penultimate line of
this terrifying poem includes not only the speaker and the

"thoroughbred mental cases" inside the hospital, but the reader as well.

Ordinary physical ailments are always seen as significant of a more profound mental or spiritual disorder. In "Night Sweat," for example, the speaker suffers from a transient episode of fever, but as he feels "the creeping damp / float over my pajamas' / wilted white," it seems as if "my life's fever is soaking in night sweat" (*FUD*, 68). Or again, the poet of "During Fever," still shaky from a recent bout of mental illness, reads his own condition into the routine childhood illness of his baby daughter:

> All night the crib creaks;
> home from the healthy country to the sick city,
> my daughter in fever
> flounders in her chicken-colored sleeping bag.
> "Sorry," she mumbles like her dim-bulb father,
>   "sorry."   [*LS*, 79]

Particularly painful are those images relating to man's attempt to ward off disease. Mother Lowell relies on her "electric blanket" and "silver hot water bottle"; the poet and his wife are "Tamed by *Miltown*" (*LS*, 80, 87); in the city hospital, the patients are "plugged to jugs of dim blue doctored water" (*Nbk*, 230). Perhaps the most bizarre medical image in *Notebook* refers to a goiter test given to the poet, a test which seems less a prelude to cure than a nightmare in which the doctors steal the patient's health:

> On a second floor in a second hospital
> two racoons wear stethoscopes to count the pulse
> of their geiger-counter and their thyroid scan;
> they sit sipping my radioactive iodine
> from a small lead bottle with two metal straws,
> "What little health we have is stolen fruit."   [137–138]

The treatment of disease is often more frightening than the disease itself, for it is impersonal, incomprehensible, and somehow sinister in its remoteness from the human being who is its subject and victim.

Graveyard. From the prison and the hospital it is only a short step to the graveyard. Lowell's lyric speaker wanders through the city of death, contemplating gravestones, coffins, and hearses. Irrelevantly, he surveys his tiny townhouse garden and notes that "a choreman tends our coffin's length of soil" (*LS,* 84). Or, reading his new book of poems and wondering whether it will earn him "a pass to the minor slopes of Parnassus," he sardonically refers to his poetic works as "the corpse of . . . insect lives preserved in honey" and compares his open book to an "open coffin" (*Nbk,* 213). Even in *Imitations,* in which Lowell is translating, however freely, the work of other poets, death and the grave provide the subject of roughly one-third of the poems, including "The Killing of Lykaeon" (Homer), "The Great Testament" (Villon), the elegies on Gautier by Hugo and Mallarmé, both of which Lowell calls "At Gautier's Grave," "A Roman Sarcophagus" (Rilke), and "The Sleeper in the Valley" (Rimbaud).

In the early poetry, Lowell dwells on death with a certain degree of *schadenfreude;* the grave is the place where his Calvinistic ancestors are punished for their sins, where the "disgraced" must "face Jehovah's buffets and his ends" (*LWC,* 54). In "At the Indian Killer's Grave," for example, Lowell castigates the Pilgrims, whose inhumane religion and cruel politics were, he feels, responsible for the death of the Indian King Philip: "The libertarian crown / Of England built their mausoleum. Here / A clutter of Bible and weeping willows guards / The stern Colonial magistrates." Similarly, in "Dunbarton," the poet implies that his ancestors, the "half-forgotten Starks and Winslows" who "fill / The granite plot," deserve their death because they represent a desiccated Puritanism. Not even his own grandfather, recently dead, is mourned by the poet; on the contrary, the dead man "Chatters to nothing in the thankless ground / His father screwed from Charlie Stark" (*LWC,* 55, 20, 24). In "The Quaker Graveyard in Nantucket," the whole Atlantic becomes one vast cemetery for those "blue sailors" like the poet's cousin Warren Winslow, whose participation in World War II somehow relates them to the materialistic, unbelieving Quakers of New England.

In *Life Studies,* similar graveyard images occur but in a radically altered context: the dead are now pitied and mourned rather than scolded. In "Dunbarton," for example, the poet fondly recalls the "yearly get-aways from Boston / to the family graveyard in Dunbarton" which he shared with his grandfather during his childhood. The duty of tending the family graves became a rite of love: "Grandfather and I / raked leaves from our dead forbears, / defied the dank weather / with 'dragon' bonfires" (66). Again, the corpse of his mother, "wrapped like *panetone* in Italian tin foil," is contemplated with a mixture of awe and pity; the pomp and circumstance of her *"Risorgimento* black and gold casket" is sadly out of date (78, 77).

"The Flaw" in *For the Union Dead* is perhaps the first poem in which death is seen as something that happens not only to other people but also to oneself. Driving past a little country graveyard with his wife, the poet gets a speck in his eye, and his fractured vision transforms the gravestones that he sees into his own tomb:

> Old wives and husbands! Look, their gravestones wait
> in couples with the names and half the date—
> one future and one freedom. In a flash,
> I see us whiten into skeletons,
> our eager, sharpened cries, a pair of stones,
> cutting like shark-fins through the boundless wash.   [66]

In *Notebook,* the fear of personal death becomes more and more acute. Having to teach after "less than three hours' sleep," the poet knows that his body must pay the price, that his "gray hairs will not go down to the grave in peace." Like the Aztec woman, abandoned by her husband, who sings her "adultery ballads," he knows he must face "the poverty all men must face at the hour of death" (88, 104). Increasingly, the poet stresses the lesson of humility:

> Each night I lie me down to sleep in rest;
> two or three times a week, I wake to my sin. . . .
> God himself cannot wake up five years younger,
> and drink away the chalice of our death-sentence . . .
>
> [*Nbk,* 199]

When the poet of *Notebook* closes his eyes, trying to imagine the street scenes of New York City half a century ago, he hears the "clopping / of the hundreds of horses unstopping" and notices with horror that "each hauls a coffin" (260). In Lowell's imaginary world, cars turn out to be hearses, gardens are measured by coffin lengths, and the function of horses is to haul coffins. The noisy, chaotically energetic city is the dead land: "frayed flags / quilt the graveyard of the Grand Army of the Republic" (*FUD,* 71).

The Perspective of History

> always inside me is the child who died . . .
> "Night Sweat"

Lowell's world, as I have described it so far, seems to be one of unremitting ugliness, pain, and death—a world of frozen cats, frayed flags quilting graveyards, fatigued elm leaves, and discarded metal containers. Yet in the very act of remembering the precise quality of former sensations and emotions, and in relating past to present, the poet asserts his consciousness of self, conferring upon the bleak items of his landscape a palpable, authentic existence, an oddly unexpected radiance. Like Yeats, Lowell creates a mythology out of his own life and those of his friends, relatives, or historical counterparts.

Before discussing the recurrent references to time, place, and person in Lowell's total work, let us look closely at the use of temporal and spatial perspectives in a single poem. I have chosen "To Delmore Schwartz" (*LS* 53–54) an occasional poem generally considered one of the less successful lyrics in *Life Studies*.[13] Many of the kinds of imagery discussed in the preceding sections are found in this poem: pollution ("the antiquated refrigerator gurgled mustard gas," "the room was filled / with cigarette smoke"); dead metal ("a tin wastebasket of rum," "You must have propped its eyelids with a nail"); hand and foot imagery ("its brow / was high and thinner than a baby's thumb," "its webs were tough as toe nails on its bough"); disease (" our universal / *Angst*," "the paranoid, / inert gaze of Coleridge," "Stalin has had two cerebral hemorrhages"); and death ("it looked through us, as if it'd died dead drunk," "It was your first kill," the "inert gaze of Coleridge"). But despite this emphasis on decay, disease, and death, "To Delmore Schwartz" is less a depressing poem than a loving one. We must look at the role of its persons and places and at its temporal perspective to see why this is so.

The poem records an incident in the past from the vantage point of the present. The very fact that the poet wishes to remind his friend and fellow poet of a particular evening in such vivid detail implies that both have outgrown the frame of mind depicted in the poem. The speaker who ruefully recalls that "We couldn't even keep the furnace lit!" is, of course, no longer "nobly mad"; he now discriminates quite calmly between various impressions, recalling with great care the relationship of the objects in the room, the conversation, the appearance of the Charles river at dawn. The "I" of the present expresses no bitterness toward the remembered past, no anger at his former life. On the contrary, the act of remembering, of bringing the past to life, compensates for his former pain. With ironic and amused detachment, the speaker recalls the self-doubt and insecurity of the fledgling artist he once was. And the implication of the direct address is that Delmore too can now laugh at his former self.

The number of proper names in "To Delmore Schwartz" is unusually large, and indeed it seems that repeated allusions to persons and places play the central role in defining the sensibilities of the two protagonists. The scene is a "mustard-yellow" house in the shadow of Harvard, but although the two young poets are acutely, indeed self-consciously, aware of their literary heritage, theirs is hardly the Cambridge of serious intellectual pursuit. The opening lines present an image of comic disorder:

> We couldn't even keep the furnace lit!
> Even when we had disconnected it,
> the antiquated
> refrigerator gurgled mustard gas.

The furnace that should gurgle is dead; the refrigerator that should be dead gurgles. Because of this foolish domestic crisis, the anticipated "literary evening" does not come off. But what sort of literary evening was it to be? The guest whom Lowell and Schwartz had "long maneuvered" to invite is not T. S. Eliot himself, but only the Master's brother Henry Ware, whose name, oddly evocative of "hardware," suggests that the two young men are still a long way from Parnassus.

Abruptly the narrator now shifts to the image of the stuffed duck, Delmore's "first kill," which is ironically the only "Rabelaisian" spirit at the poet's gathering, the only member of the party who "craned [note the witty pun] toward Harvard." Perched on Lowell's "trunk and typing table" (the implication is that no typing is ever done in this milieu), the dead duck "looked through us"; its quixotic open-eyed stare is paradoxically the most alive thing in the room and challenges the diffidence and inertia of the two young men. The stability of its presence relieves their "universal / *Angst* a moment," and after a few drinks, they become "Underseas fellows, nobly mad," defying "the chicken-hearted shadows of the world." With fine bravado, Delmore now invokes the spirits of Joyce and Freud; punning on their names, he calls them "the Masters of Joy." But of course, as Delmore knows, Joyce and Freud, the two archetypal "great minds" of the early twentieth century, are anything but masters of joy. On the contrary, it is they who introduced the new age of self-consciousness and *Angst* from which the protagonists of the poem seem to be suffering. Therefore, the invocation of Joyce and Freud does not brighten the poets' spirits; immediately their attention shifts to the "paranoid / inert gaze of Coleridge, back / from Malta" —the gaze of the *poète maudit,* painted at the turning point of his life when he knew there was no escape from drug addiction.

This bitter image of Coleridge is followed by an equally bitter version of Wordsworth: Delmore purposely misquotes the famous lines from "Resolution and Independence," substituting "sadness" for "gladness": "We poets in our youth begin in sadness;/thereof in the end come despondency and madness." [14] He rejects, in other words, Wordsworth's conviction that a "peculiar grace" can restore the poet to the primal joy which is his birthright. On the contrary, the poet's permanent condition is one of *angst*—his counterpart of Stalin's "cerebral hemorrhages." No wonder that the only joyful member of the party is the tiger kitten Oranges, and even he "cartwheeled for joy in a ball of snarls."

Although Lowell's strategy is extremely devious, it becomes apparent by the end of the poem that the seemingly random use of proper names actually serves a particular function. The fledgling poets are presented as an ironic version of Wordsworth and Coleridge, a Wordsworth and Coleridge who have lost the spontaneous creative impulse because the age of Freud and Joyce has intervened, making

Wordsworth's "gladness" somehow obsolete. Inheritors of Coleridge's paranoia and of Wordsworth's despondency rather than of their poetic genius, the two drinkers become more and more inert as the evening wears on. Having been rebuffed even by Henry Ware, they retreat into the "chicken-hearted shadows." As the poem ends, their one and only attempt to *act* is recalled by the narrator:

> The Charles
> River was turning silver. In the ebb-
> light of morning, we stuck
> the duck
> -s web-
> foot, like a candle, in a quart of gin we'd killed.

The breaking up of words and syllables at line ends, the strong caesurae, the falling rhythm ("Ríver was túrning sílver"), and harsh rhyme ("struck" / "duck") underline the comic futility of this absurd action. Reduced to total passivity, the two young men can do nothing but kill the already dead duck a second time.

The allusions to persons and places, as well as the perspective of the present on the past, give this relatively short poem an astonishing range of implication. The juxtaposition of the dead duck's "Rabelaisian" "stare" to Coleridge's "paranoid / inert gaze," for example, comically punctuates the earnestness and sense of self-importance of young Lowell and Schwartz. The mature poet can look back at this neurotic phase of his career with some equanimity; his ironic awareness tempers the pain.

Persons and Places. We are now in a better position to understand the role of the recurrent references to persons, places, and time in Lowell's universe. By establishing a particular historical context for his poetic "events," the poet gives an ironic edge to the despair that is the source of so much of his imagery.

The allusions to persons in "To Delmore Schwartz" are typical not only of *Life Studies* but of Lowell's poetry in general. Essentially an autobiographical poet, Lowell rarely invents fictional characters, and those who do appear in his poetry—Anne Kavanaugh, the "Mad Negro Soldier Confined at Munich," or the New Brunswick nun of "Mother Marie Therese"—seem rather transparent masks for Lowell himself.[15] In general, Lowell's personae fall into three categories: relatives and personal friends, writers and artists, and historical figures. The third group is perhaps the least interesting. When Lowell portrays great rulers past and present, he rarely avoids a slightly shrill invective. Thus in *Notebook,* the Duc de Guise is portrayed as a "warhawk" with a "drugged bull's breathing, a cool, well-pastured brain"; Charles V "carried enemies with him in a cage" (46, 166); Attila "never entered a house that wasn't burning"; and the life of El Presidente Leoni of Venezuela depends upon "his small men with 18- / inch repeating pistols, firing 45 bullets a minute" (162, 53). Violence and the lust for power—these are traits repeatedly singled out for comment. Stalin, for example, made his way to the top because "The large stomach could only chew success. What raised him / was the usual lust to break the icon, / joke cruelly, seriously, and be himself" (208). The irony of this statement (Stalin can "be himself" only by being a murderer) is surely heavy-handed, and one feels that the poet is, in Yeatsian vocabulary, quarreling with others rather than with himself and hence producing rhetoric rather than poetry.

When dealing with a historical figure like Colonel Robert Shaw, the commander of the first all-Negro regiment in the Civil War, Lowell is guilty of the opposite kind of oversimplification—nostalgic sentimentality. Colonel Shaw "has an angry wrenlike vigilance, / a greyhound's gentle tautness; / he seems to wince at pleasure, / and suffocate for privacy" (*FUD,* 71). It follows that he is "out of bounds

now," that in the rapacious commercial world of the twentieth century, his heroism is irrelevant. Here again the contrast between Shaw's devoted service to the state and our
modern "savage servility" that "slides by on grease" seems
facile.

Lowell's portraits of fellow writers are much more objec-
tively rendered; as in the case of "To Delmore Schwartz," he
focuses on the revealing gesture, expression, or physical trait,
deriving larger meanings from the concrete instance. In contemplating other writers, the poet is repeatedly surprised by
the ironic gap between creative genius and the everyday per-
sonality, between the inner spark and the outer manner.
Ford Madox Ford, for example, whose *Good Soldier* was
considered "the best French novel in the language," is presented as a ludicrous old man, a "mammoth mumbler," with
"fish-blue eyes, and mouth pushed out, /fish-fashion" (*LS*, 49,
50). William Carlos Williams, the poet who celebrated life
in its most diverse forms, is glimpsed as the most ordinary of
ailing old men, "straying stonefoot through his town-end
garden, / man and flower seedy with three autumn strokes"
(*Nbk,* 121). Theodore Roethke, who "honored nature" in its
elemental simplicity, was himself a "Sheeplike, unsociable,
reptilian" creature (*Nbk,* 202). Especially poignant is the
portrait of Robert Frost, having just received a tremendous
ovation at a poetry reading, admitting to the young Robert
Lowell that both his children suffer from mental illness: " 'I
think / how little good my health did anyone near me' "
(*Nbk,* 122). In all these portraits, the tone is totally without
condescension because the poet judges himself no less se-
verely than he judges others. This is particularly true of the
poems in *For the Union Dead:* "Tenth Muse," "Myopia: a
Night," "Eye and Tooth," and "Child's Song" present the
middle-aged poet in all his weakness, sloth, hypochondria,
and cowardice. "Sometimes," the speaker wryly remarks, "the
little muddler / can't stand himself" (22).

Lowell's family poems have puzzled many critics. When

Life Studies first appeared, Joseph Bennett complained in the *Hudson Review* that the "whole volume is a collection of lazily recollected and somewhat snobbish memoirs, principally of the poet's own wealthy and aristocratic family." [16] This is surely to miss the point. From *Land of Unlikeness* on, Lowell has presented those "Mayflower screwballs" (*LS*, 82), the Starks, Winslows, and Lowells who are his ancestors, as representative victims of the American dream. Self-righteous, hard-working, materialistic, and clannish, they built a Beacon Hill and a Maine empire that was fated to crumble. Edward Winslow, who came over on the Mayflower and became governor of Plymouth, his grandson Edward, sheriff and silversmith, and General John Stark, the Revolutionary War general who founded the township of Dunbarton—all successful men of their day—are succeeded by equally practical and materialistic but less accomplished Winslows like Ancrem, collector of blue china, and Arthur Winslow, the poet's maternal grandfather, a kindly but success-ridden speculator who ultimately lost his millions in "Boston real estate" (*LWC*, 18, 21), a man whose decor, lovingly described in "My Last Afternoon with Uncle Devereux Winslow," was "manly, comfortable, / overbearing, disproportioned" (*LS*, 60). Arthur Winslow's children represent a further decline: Devereux dies of Hodgkin's disease at the age of twenty-nine; Sarah, a neurasthenic spinster, lives in a dream world in which she appears in Symphony Hall as a great concert pianist (*LS*, 61–63); and Charlotte, the poet's mother, "still her Father's daughter," finds solace in "new / caps on all her teeth," and her "electric blanket" (*LS*, 70, 71, 80). Her hopelessly deadlocked marriage to Commander Lowell and its effects on young Bob is the central theme of *Life Studies*. It continues to obsess the poet in *For The Union Dead* (7), and in the "Five Dreams" sequence of *Notebook* he wonders which of his parents was the more guilty.

The Stark-Winslow-Lowell family thus plays an important

thematic role throughout Lowell's poetry. This family, like Faulkner's Sartoris and Compson families, represents a culture that is now in decline, but that at least embodies a meaningful tradition. Much less integral are the references to the poet's daughter Harriet in *Notebook*. Harriet, in her nursery bed "manned by a madhouse of stuffed animals," or castigating her father for not voting for Humphrey on November 6, 1967, or coming home from Camp Alamoosook (21, 231, 239) is meant to be the archetypal poet's child, but the image remains vague and sentimentalized because, unlike Arthur Winslow or Commander Lowell, Harriet does not represent a particular class, profession, culture, or complex of values. The treatment of the Harriet figure reminds us how difficult it is to create such superb Lowell personae as the Jonathan Edwards who addresses Josiah Hawley (*LWC*, 59), or the Commander Lowell of "Terminal Days at Beverly Farms" (*LS*, 73)—characters at once wholly individual and yet representative of a larger moral scheme.

What has been said of persons in Lowell's poetry is equally true of places, and it would be tedious to catalogue the countless references to Cape Cod, Central Park, Boylston Street, Dunbarton, or Third Avenue. If one were to draw a map of the Lowell country, one would begin with the Boston Common and the Statehouse as one's center (*LWC*, 25, 55; *FUD*, 70), move outward to Cambridge past the Public Gardens and the Union Boat Club, to Harvard and M.I.T., and onward to Brockton, Beverly Farms, Salem, Concord, Dunbarton, and finally Maine. In Lowell's later volumes, the Boston scene gives way to New York—the New York of wafer balconies, windows that suggest prison cells, the dirty rowboats of Central Park, the "tundra . . . past Eightieth Street to Sixty-Seventh," the "Nineteenth Century Capitalistic Gothic" of Central Park West (*Nbk*, 110, 260). From the center of Manhattan, the poet moves past the West Side Drive to the polluted Hudson, or he travels eastward to the giant airports of Long Island, whose jets will drop him in Brazil or in the Hotel Continental of Buenos Aires, with its "false fin de siecle decorum" (*FUD*, 10, 62, 60).

The references to place are not important for their own sake but again function in the larger context of the poem. In "For George Santayana," the speaker recalls the dying days of the "free-thinking Catholic infidel" in the monastery hospital of Santo Stefano:

> Later I used to dawdle
> past Circus and Mithraic Temple
> to Santo Stefano grown paper-thin
> like you from waiting . . .
>
> [*LS*, 51; spaced dots, Lowell's]

The place references in this passage have a documentary accuracy: the poet makes his way from downtown Rome past the Circus Maximus and one of the Mithraic temples of the Forum, to Santo Stefano Rotondo in the outskirts of Rome. But it is a symbolic journey as well. The Mithraic religion —the worship of the God of light—posed a major threat to Christianity in the first centuries after Christ. Like Santayana, whose search for light rejected a Christianity to which he was nonetheless emotionally bound, the poet flirts with pagan myth and religion ("I used to dawdle / past Circus and Mithraic Temple") before coming round to the Christian church built for Stephen Protomartyr. Like St. Stephen, Santayana is a martyr to his cause: he is finally alone in the "worn arena" of his magnifying glass (his version of the Circus Maximus), where the "whirling sand / and broken-hearted lions lick his hand." Here and elsewhere, Lowell's place names have a central function in defining the larger meaning of the poem in which they occur.

"The Jerking Noose of Time." I have saved until last Lowell's treatment of temporal relationships—the repeated

reference to hours, days, months, and years, and to the inter-
vals between given points in time, to precise ages and dates
and to the calendar and clock—because time imagery is perhaps more central to Lowell's poetic imagination than any
other group of images I have discussed. Consider the following examples:

> the year,
> The nineteen-hundred forty-fifth of grace,
> Lumbers with losses up the clinkered hill
> Of our purgation. [*LWC*, 4]

> These sixteen centuries, Eternal City,
> That we have squandered since Maxentius fell
> Under the Milvian Bridge. [*LWC*, 49]

> *September twenty-second*, Sir: today
> I answer. In the latter part of May,
> Hard on our Lord's Ascension, it began
> To be more sensible. [*LWC*, 60]

> There, just a month before
> Our marriage, I can see you. [*MK*, 9]

> Then you were grown; I left you on your own.
> We will forget that August twenty-third,
> When Mother motored with the maids to Stowe . . .
> [*MK*, 31]

> Forty years earlier,
> twenty, auburn headed,
> grasshopper notes of genius! [*LS*, 62]

> In 1911, he had stopped growing at just six feet.
> [*LS*, 64]

> It's easy to tick
> off the minutes,
> but the clockhands stick. [*FUD*, 12]

> The vaporish closeness of this two-month fog;
> thirty-five summers back, the brightest summer.
> [*Nbk*, 26]

last 4 A.M. to 7, I lay awake,
my mouth watering for some painless poison.

[*Nbk,* 161]

Always the sound thirty-five years we've lost.

[*Nbk,* 226]

Lowellian time is extremely hard to define even though many critics have noted the poet's preoccupation with the past, his consciousness of history, his dialogue with his "ancestral voices." [17] Yet Lowell's sense of the past is not Romantic; unlike Wordsworth, he does not yearn for a lost paradise; unlike Eliot, he does not remind us of a heroic past which will atone for the sordidness of the present. The past, as we have seen in the case of "To Delmore Schwartz," is rarely less ugly, unpleasant, or agonizing than the present, and Randall Jarrell quite rightly observed in his essay on the early poetry of Lowell that it is the "fundamental likeness of the past and present and not their disparity, which is insisted upon." [18]

If the present depends totally on the past, then perhaps time is a meaningless continuum leading nowhere. Geoffrey Hartman implies as much when he argues that "Lowell's attitude toward time is paradoxical: time is the accuser, yet time is inauthentic. Time eyes us through objects that loom large, or through 'unforgivable' landscapes, yet everything converges to no effect, like waves breaking harmlessly and sight blurring." [19]

In other words, for Lowell there is no future and no eternity—only a present which contains the pressure of a recollected past. But the past is not therefore imprisoning, as it is, say, for Henry James. In a brilliant analysis, Georges Poulet has shown that despite James's professed "delight in a palpable imaginable *visitable* past—in nearer distances and the clearer mysteries," [20] he actually feared the past because the mass of remembered images tended to stifle his consciousness of the present. In order to circumvent the loss of self in the multiplicity of memories, James divested his characters of all but their most shallow immediate past; compared, say, to Tolstoy's characters, they have astonishingly little duration. "To go from Europe to America or from America to Europe implies in this regard a more significant mutation than to pass from adolescence to manhood." [21] Time, in other words, gives way to space.

Lowell's sense of the past has been called "Jamesian," [22] but it is in fact quite different. The self has duration; the poet's method, which we have already observed in "To Delmore Schwartz," is to confer authenticity on the present by linking it to the past. He is thus able to stand outside his own history and to evaluate it with some ironic detachment. Lowell's Jonathan Edwards, his Uncle Devereux, or for that matter his Robert Lowell, have a past and present existence rarely found in lyric poetry. In this regard, Lowell's method is closer to Chekhov's or Flaubert's than to that of most lyric poets.

Because his sensibility is basically elegiac, the apocalyptic voice that Lowell assumes in some of his early poems sounds shrill and hollow. The visionary mode of a Blake or a Rimbaud is alien to him. In "Christmas Eve under Hooker's Statue," for example, he shifts uneasily from historical narrative to prophecy, from the comparison of the Civil War and World War II ("Tonight a blackout") to the sudden vision of freedom, open fields, and a Christ "once again turned wanderer and child" (*LWC,* 17). Memory and prophetic vision similarly fail to cohere in "The First Sunday in Lent." The poem begins in the present as the speaker, at his attic window on a slushy March Sunday morning in Boston, surveys "the well-born stamp / From sermons in a scolded, sober mob" (*LWC,* 15). Their empty religious rites recall his childhood days in the attic where he had once hidden his "stolen agates and the cannister / preserved from Bunker Hill."

These Civil War toys were, the poem implies, the fruits of the Protestant American materialism described in the first stanza, a commercialism that defeated the agrarian South.

The present is thus seen as an outgrowth of the past, but in the third stanza the narrative breaks down as the poet suddenly recalls the doom of Troy—a doom somehow equivalent to that of war-torn America, unless man can be renewed through grace as an "unblemished Adam." The jump from concrete incident to prophetic warning is too sudden; there is a hiatus between remembered incident and apocalyptic vision.

The thrust to be taken outside time to eternity ("Gospel me to the Garden"; "O Mary, marry earth, sea, air and fire" [*LWC*, 57, 68]), only intermittently present in *Lord Weary's Castle,* is absent from Lowell's later poetry, and indeed even in *Lord Weary's Castle* the sense of the actual passage of time is already obsessive as can be seen from the openings of many of the poems:

> This Easter, Arthur Winslow, five years gone
> I came to mourn you, not to praise the craft
> That netted you a million dollars . . .   [21]

> When we were children our papas were stout
> And colorless as seaweed.   [18]

> Meeting his mother makes him lose ten years,
> Or is it twenty?   [41]

> Thanksgiving night: Third Avenue was dead.   [*MK,* 51]

The exploration of time past is the central preoccupation of *Life Studies.* In "Grandparents" (68), for example, the speaker, a lonely middle-aged man, learns to understand himself by coming to terms with the lost world of his grandparents. At the beginning of the poem, he is faintly contemptuous of those now "altogether otherworldly" adults who made their ritual "champing" descent on "pharmacist

and five-and-ten in Brockton" every Friday, buying up goods
to preserve their self-imposed isolation on their farm for at
least one more week. Foolishly authoritarian Grandpa
thought he could police his little world by waving a cane at
one and all, while Grandmother merely retreated in mock
Mohammedan fashion, behind "her thick / lavender mourning and touring veil." "Mourning and touring"—the parallel construction and eye rhyme point up the "otherworldly"
ineffectuality of those who equate these two activities.

But what is the identity of the "I" who, having dismissed
these "nineteenth-century" "children" as wholly irrelevant,
has inherited their farm? The long summer season, perhaps
misused by his Grandparents, is a mere vacuum for him; he
continues to live in a past which is characterized by the
strains of "Summer Time" heard on the "rattley little country gramophone / racking its five-foot horn," a relic of the
Ancien Régime world of his grandparents. As his eye falls
on the green billiards-table, however, a sudden memory dis-
sipates his passive mood:

> no field is greener than its cloth,
> where Grandpa, dipping sugar for us both,
> once spilled his demitasse.
> His favorite ball, the number three,
> still hides the coffee stain.

The memory of this trivial incident puts Grandpa in a totally different light. It is not the old man's pretentious futility that is now remembered but his capacity for love.
Grandpa's fussy little gesture ("dipping sugar for us both")
may be regarded as a kind of communion whose memory
makes the green cloth of the billiards-table greener than the
meadows of a lost Eden. The vision of Grandpa's favorite
ball, "the number three," which "still hides the coffee stain,"
brings back in an instant of joy the whole casually happy
aura of Lowell's childhood summers on the farm.

But the moment of joy does not last, for now the poet must suddenly come to terms emotionally with what he has known only rationally thus far: his grandfather is dead, there will be no more billiard games. The line, "Grandpa! Have me, hold me, cherish me!" sounds sentimental out of context, but the real pathos is that the speaker knows, even as tears "smut" his fingers, that he cannot change his own neurotically divided response to Grandpa: the battle with the dead will continue:

> half my life-lease later,
> I hold an *Illustrated London News*——;
> disloyal still,
> I doodle handlebar
> mustaches on the last Russian Czar.

The musty old copy of the *Illustrated London News* with its anachronistic photograph of the last Czar is an appropriate image for the decaying world of Lowell's grandparents. As such, the poet can neither ignore it nor treat it with respect. Half a "life-lease later," he must continue to deface it, to negate the childhood world he really loves.

The poem thus moves toward the touching recognition of the speaker's divided loyalties; it presents an ironic image of the poet's own repeated attempts at disloyalty to a tradition which has, in fact, shaped his life. The span of adolescence was not a "throw away" after all. Fifty years later, it *still* (the word "still" appears five times in the poem) controls the present. And only by coming to terms with his past can the poet know himself.

Throughout *For the Union Dead,* memory similarly illuminates an often confusing present. In "Eye and Tooth," the memory of real pain puts the throbbing of the "old cut cornea" in its proper perspective. How boring, the poem suggests, one's minor complaints are—not only to others but even to oneself! In *Notebook,* there is hardly a poem that does not refer to the "passage from lower to upper middle age" (256), to the "brown hours" that "stream like water off my back" (82), to the minutes, days, and months that make up human existence. The poet's status as a man of some fifty-odd years is a frequent point of reference. The "I" is given to waking up early in the morning after a restless night, to "sing the dawnless alba of the gerontoi" (140). In the middle of a sleepless night, he wonders how he will survive the "four-hour stay till morning," or how he will teach the next day on "less than three hours' sleep" (88). As in *Life Studies,* figures from the past haunt his thoughts:

> They won't stay gone, rising with royal torpor
> as if held in my binoculars' fog and enlargement,
> casting the raindrops of the rainbow: children;
> loved by their still older elders in a springtide
> invisible to us as the Hittites.
>
> ["Those Older," Sonnet 1, *Nbk,* 123]

In the "Five Dreams" sequence (41–43), the poet relives the endless battles between his parents; in the "Charles River" sonnets (66–70), he recalls a painful college love affair, destroyed by his father's interference.

The first sonnet in *Notebook* is typical of the whole collection; it humorously exposes the futility of the human urge to measure, define, and order one's existence. Just as the poet's daughter has tried, year after year, to arrive at a proper conception of God until, at the grand old age of ten and a half, she gives up the whole thing, so the poet makes a useless ritual of getting somewhere, of having a purpose: "For / the hundredth time, I slice through fog, and round / the village with my headlights on the ground, / as if I were the first philosopher" (21). Like his daughter, he is looking for The Answer but it eludes him: the lost car key does not miraculously appear "behind the next crook in the road." Meanwhile the moon, seen by the time-ridden poet as a "face, clock-white," is the one constant timepiece in his changing universe. Even though it is "blinded" by the "feeble beams" of his headlights, it is "still friendly to the earth."

It is this kind of ironic detachment that characterizes Lowell's sense of time past throughout the *Notebook* sonnets. In "The Golden Middle," for example, the speaker ruefully contemplates the trappings of middle-aged literary success: an oak-paneled library with "book ladders on brass rods and rollers." But such comfort exacts a high price: gone is the passionate involvement of youth, of the young student "graced with rebellion, hair and the caw of Shelley" (*Nbk,* 131). "The Golden Middle" turns out to be that in-between time of life when one still envies the young Shelleys but knows that to remain alive means to renounce the "hard, cunning light" of youthful genius. "Who can deduct these years?" the poet asks, knowing that, given the choice between life and the "ignominious and bitter death" of a Shelley, he would opt for life.

Lowell's sense of the transformations wrought by time, as well as of the basic continuity behind them, is unerring. From the ringing denunciation of the violence of the "nineteen-hundred forty-fifth [year] of grace" (*LWC,* 4) to the pained acceptance of the "tranquillized fifties" (*LS,* 85) and the puzzled contemplation of the "going generation" of the frantic sixties (*Nbk,* 241), Lowell has created a powerful image of America in the latter half of the twentieth century, a country that has evolved from, but is no longer recognizable as "the old United States of William James, / its plaintive, now arthritic optimism," a world a long way from "Sunday mahjong and netting butterflies" (*Nbk,* 241, 190).

"Whenever I read a poem by Robert Lowell," Elizabeth Bishop has remarked, "I have a chilling sensation of here-and-now, of exact contemporaneity; more aware of those 'ironies of American history,' grimmer about them, and yet hopeful." [23] The imaginative structure of Lowell's poetic world, as I have tried to define it, depends precisely on the complex response to history which Bishop notes. The bitter response to the decay, noise, violence, and spiritual malaise of our world is tempered by the humanist's consciousness of his own destiny as it unfolds in time. The poet's terror during the "one dark night" of "Skunk Hour", a night that he must live over and over again, is transcended in those moments when he recognizes that the act of remembering—even when the events and emotions recalled are such painful ones—is a source of illumination and hope.

Chapter Two

The Limits of Imitation:
Robert Lowell's Rimbaud

In the preceding chapter, I argued that Lowell's imaginative universe has a highly articulated structure. But this very consistency and precision of reference may prove to be a disadvantage to the lyric poet who turns translator, especially when he chooses to translate poems whose network of images is equally systematic but entirely different from his own. *Imitations* (1961) thus has a problematic place in the Lowell canon.

Why, to begin with, does Lowell call his poetic translations "imitations"? Is he in fact writing original poems based loosely on poems by such major European poets as Baudelaire and Rilke? The continuing, and often heated, debate on the relative merits of *Imitations* reflects a certain confusion about Lowell's aims and achievements, a confusion for which Lowell himself is surely partially responsible. In his Introduction to *Imitations,* he explains: "This book is partly self-sufficient and separate from its sources, and should be first read as a sequence, one voice running through many personalities, contrasts and repetitions. . . . I have been reckless with literal meaning, and labored hard to get the tone. Most often this has been *a* tone, for *the* tone is something that will always more or less escape transference to another language and cultural moment. I have tried to write

55

alive English and to do what my authors might have done if they were writing their poems now and in America." [1]

Taking this statement at face value, critics have made extravagant claims for *Imitations*. "*Not* a book of translations," A. Alvarez insisted in an early review, "it is a magnificent collection of new poems by Robert Lowell, based on the work of 18 European poets. . . . A new development in that constantly expanding imaginative universe in which Lowell orbits. . . . The most varied and moving book that this leader of mid-century poetry has yet produced." [2] In the same vein, Edmund Wilson declared that "Lowell, who has used material from a variety of other writers, all the way from Homer to Pasternak, has produced a volume of verse which consists of variations on themes provided by those other poets and which is really an original sequence by Robert Lowell of Boston." [3] And Irvin Ehrenpreis has observed that "far from losing himself in the character of the author whose work he translates, Lowell deliberately extends his identity to the other man." *Imitations* is a "sequence rather than a miscellaneous collection," a sequence in which the poet "is legitimising his progeny, replacing the Lowells and Winslows by Baudelaire, Rimbaud and Rilke." [4]

The view that Lowell's imitations are "ontologically complete," [5] that they can be read as independent and original poems, has been hotly contested by other critics, most notably John Simon, who argues that whereas the medieval "imitator" (for example, Chaucer in *Troilus and Criseyde*) took a story or poem by a "maker" in some foreign language and retold it freely in his native tongue, Lowell not only borrows plots, themes, and characters, but tends to translate the parent text line by line, adhering to its overall structure, imagery, and diction. As such, Lowell must be judged on his merits as a translator, and Simon finds no justification for his occasional cuts, additions, and transpositions: "Does a translator—even if he calls himself by another name, such as 'imitator,' supposed to set him beyond the reach of criticism —have the right to change the entire mood, intention, import of a poem? . . . At what point does an act of 'imitation' become an immoral act?" [6]

Whether or not Lowell has the "right to change" the mood and intention of the poems he translates seems to me beside the point; the real issue is not the morality of Lowell's verse translations, or lack of it, but their aesthetic value. What I propose to do here is first to examine one of Lowell's imitations as if it were an entirely original poem and only then to compare it to the parent text. This procedure may clarify some of the problems inherent in translation.

My text is "Nostalgia," an imitation of Rimbaud's "Mémoire." * I have chosen a Rimbaud poem because even those critics who are less than enthusiastic about Lowell's imitations have admired his versions of Rimbaud, while his advocates have used these imitations as a prime example of Lowell's poetic inventiveness. John Simon calls Rimbaud Lowell's "major kinsman"; [7] John Bayley argues that Rimbaud's much flaunted *dérèglement* "seems in accord with Lowell's own poetic temper"; [8] Richard Fein observes, "In the versions from Rimbaud we witness the child's lust for freedom, the wise boy tortured by his knowledge and a desire to escape, the weights of which we feel in Lowell's autobiographical piece '91 Revere Street' and in some of the poems from *Life Studies";* [9] and Ehrenpreis writes, "If in artistic sensibility Lowell seems peculiarly at home with Baudelaire, he seems as a person still more at ease with Rimbaud, whose work is placed at the exact centre of the book. With both poets he finds continual opportunities for employing his own tone and his imagery of passivity eager for motion. But Rimbaud brings out attitudes toward childhood and corrupted innocence that remind us at once of *Life*

---

* Both texts as well as Wallace Fowlie's literal translation of "Mémoire" are reprinted at the end of this chapter.

Studies. Mme. Rimbaud as 'Mother' inexorably recalls Mrs. Lowell." [10]

The parenthetical note placed after the title of "Nostalgia" tells us that this is an "autobiographical poem" and provides a scenario for the action. One is immediately reminded of *Life Studies*: "My Last Afternoon with Uncle Devereux Winslow," for example, begins with the epitaph, "1922: the stone porch of my Grandfather's summer house" (*LS*, 59), while the sensitive child's awareness of the unhappy relationship between his parents, to which Lowell alludes in the note, is a central theme in "Commander Lowell," "During Fever," and in the prose autobiography "91 Revere Street." The parenthetical note prepares us for the fact that "Nostalgia" is a narrative poem. It tells a story in the past tense, referring to the poet-protagonist in the third person, except for a shift in lines 15–16 ("Oh Bride, your faith was purer than gold coins, / marsh marigolds, my hot and burning eyelid . . .") and in section v which is entirely in the first person. The immediate subject of the autobiographical narrative is Monsieur Rimbaud's desertion of his family; the function of the river scene is to convey, in a series of images, the causes of this desertion as well as the suffering it brought both to the mother and to the child who is the future poet.

The use of the pathetic fallacy in the first line immediately suggests that childhood is remembered by the narrator not as a lost paradise but as a time of intense pain. The lazy little river in its pastoral setting becomes in the poet's imagination a threatening force, "sucking" him downward to oblivion. The "child's salt tears" were not accidental: they were a reaction to his mother's neurotic response to life. For example, she "had the blue sky for parasol, / yet begged the arched bridge and the hills for shade." She wanted, in other words, to hide from the sun, to put walls between herself and the light. "Stiffly" moving, "cold and black," she vented her animosity to the world of nature by trampling on the

weeds, and asserted her iron will by forcing her little daugh-
ters to sit still on the "heraldic green," learning their prayers
from "red Morocco Missals," when they might have been
playing happily in the sunshine.

According to the poem, the mother's Puritanical tempera-
ment was responsible for the eventual flight of her husband.
Rushing in vain after "her lost man," she was left weeping
"below the parapet," full of "Nostalgia for his hairy arms."
But no one responded to her cry: "The breath / of the dry
poplars was the wind's alone." In section iv, the lost husband
is replaced by an anonymous "man in mud-caked hip-boots,"
poling a barge along the stagnant waters—a figure symbolic
of her own deathlike rigidity. Her son shared her sense of
loss and her nostalgia. His boat, its anchor stuck in the mud
at the bottom of the river, would no longer move, and he
could not reach the water or "touch / one or the other
flower" floating on the surface of the stream. The grounded
boat is a metaphor for the alienated young poet, unable to
make contact with other human beings or to participate in
the life of nature.

The theme of "Nostalgia" may thus be defined as the trau-
matic effect of a mother's neurotic behavior on her sensitive
child. As the "lidless eye" of the water fills with mud, something is lost that can never be regained. Ehrenpreis quite
rightly observes that this Mme. Rimbaud recalls the Mrs.
Lowell of *Life Studies*. She is surprisingly like the neurasthenic "Mother" of "91 Revere Street" who "used to return
frozen and thrilled from her property disputes" and spend
her Sunday morning airing out her glacial Beacon Hill
house (13, 31), the Mrs. Lowell of the autobiographical
poems, whose "voice was still electric / with a hysterical, unmarried panic," when she read bedtime stories to young
Bob, and who was "born anew / at forty," not by falling in
love but by getting "new caps on all her teeth" (70, 71).

Thematically, then, "Nostalgia" recalls Lowell's own

poems. Much of its imagery is also recognizably Lowellian. A
landscape containing a "sucking river," "abandoned lumberyards" along a riverbank, "blocks and sawdust," "dry poplars," a "man in mud-caked hip-boots," and a boat that
"stuck fast; its anchor dug for bottom" while the surrounding water "filled with mud," is reminiscent of many Lowell
poems written during the same period as "Nostalgia." The
"sucking river," for example, recalls the sea of "Water,"
which "drenched the rock / at our feet all day, / and kept
tearing away / flake after flake"; the "abandoned lumberyards" recall the "condemned freight trains" that crowd the
"unforgivable landscape" of "The Mouth of the Hudson"
(*FUD*, 4, 10); and the "dry poplars" can be related to the
"dry road dust" that "rises to whiten / the fatigued elm
leaves" in "Grandparents" (*LS*, 68). Mud and dust are peren-
nial features of Lowell's blighted urban landscape. References to both occur in the following passage from the early
poem, "Colloquy in Black Rock":

> Mud for the mole-tide harbor, mud for mouse,
> Mud for the armored Diesel fishing tubs that thud
> A year and a day to wind and tide; the dust
> Is on this skipping heart that shakes my house.   [LWC, 5]

There are other images characteristic of Lowell in "Nostalgia." In lines 3–4, he writes,. "The *Tricouleur* / hung from
the walls restored by Joan of Arc." This is an ironic reference to the decline of France's glory: on the walls once defended by St. Joan, hangs the flag of the postrevolutionary,
secular, materialistic French Republic, a republic that has
lost Joan of Arc's sense of spiritual commitment. Like the
"sucking river," the reference to the *Tricouleur* thus has unpleasant connotations; it is reminiscent of the image of a decaying Boston world in "For the Union Dead," a world in
which "frayed flags / quilt the graveyards of the Grand Army
of the Republic" (*FUD*, 71).

The fourth stanza contains references to "the river's spotted mirror" which "steamed / off to the bare sky's perfect, burning sphere" and to "my hot and burning eyelid." As I noted in Chapter One, images of burning heat—and particularly of burning eyes—recur throughout Lowell's later poetry, symbolizing the poet's death-in-life: in "Night Sweat," for example, the protagonist is suffering through a sleepless night in which his "life's fever is soaking in night sweat," and his "leaded eyelids" weigh him down (*FUD*, 68–69).

Aside from these images of dirt, decay, and pain, however, "Nostalgia" has a whole complex of images that conventionally have positive connotations: "the girls, / while lilies on white silk," "wings of an angel," "the gold stream . . . breathing the underwater amber of its reeds," "cloth of gold coverings," "gold coins," "marsh marigolds," "grass / green in the holy April moonlight," and the yellow and "cool blue" flowers, the roses and the willows of the fifth section. All these images refer to shining light, delicacy, fertility, and soft color: the white silky fabric in line 3 is like the surface of the amber gold stream in line 5 and like the sheen of the grass in the April moonlight, line 26.

But what is the relationship of the golden flowers, the blindingly white silk, and the marshy grass to the other images in the poem? Is the gold and green riverbank scene symbolic of the childhood Eden which the poet has lost because of the failure of his parents' marriage? One could, of course, write an interesting poem juxtaposing such images of lost felicity to ones of pain and ugliness, but this is not what happens in "Nostalgia." For one thing, the river is not initially associated with joy; its "sucking" waters are immediately identified with the "child's salt tears." Nor is the vision of white lilies on white silk a joyful one, for a certain sense of imprisonment is conveyed by the phrase: "His eyes were blinded by white walls." Moreover, the white silk turns out to be the cloth of the despised *Tricouleur*. In section ii, the images of gold, underwater amber, and delicate bubbles are similarly undercut by the reference to the steaming "spotted mirror" of the water's surface. Is the "burning sphere" of the sun welcome or oppressive? There is no satisfactory answer to this question, and the images remain curiously inert and ambivalent. When the despairing speaker of line 36 says that he could not touch the blue flower which "was the ash-gray water's friend," it is difficult to know whether Lowell means that the little aquatic flower, a symbol of happiness, is now beyond the speaker's reach, or whether the "cool blue," having become the "friend" of the now sinister "ash-gray" river, no longer deserves his trust. Again, we do not know what value to assign to the flower-water images.

The more one examines the structure of imagery of "Nostalgia," the clearer it becomes that there is no satisfactory relationship between the unpleasant images—sucking river, sawdust, abandoned lumberyards, mud—and those like the white silk, gold coverings, and holy April moonlight that conventionally have positive connotations. Since we are never shown the child in possession of an idyllic golden world, it is hard to understand what he has lost at the conclusion of the narrative. It seems vaguely unfortunate that "The reeds had eaten up the roses long ago," but then what was the original value of roses to the protagonist?

It is particularly hard to assign a consistent symbolic value to the nature images in "Nostalgia" because the point of view shifts back and forth from mother to child so that one often cannot tell whether a particular reaction to the landscape is that of Mme. Rimbaud or of the poet. In section iv, for example, the "Nostalgia for his hairy arms" is surely that of the mother who has, in the preceding line, "Rushed after her lost man" and who, four lines later, "wept below the parapet." But it seems quite inconsistent that the "cold and black" mother who "trampled on the weeds" and hid from the blue sky, should now have nostalgia for a man's "hairy arms" and for the "grass / green in the holy April moon-light." In the same section, the observation that "The breath / of the dry poplars was the wind's alone" may be either that of the bereaved mother or of the narrator who is recalling the scene. In this connection, the most confusing passage in the poem occurs in lines 15–16. The apostrophe "Oh Bride" is evidently addressed to the mother since no other female presence whose "faith was purer than gold coins" has been mentioned in the poem. But does the noun phrase "marsh marigolds" refer to the "gold coins" of her pure faith or to the "hot and burning eyelid" of the speaker? The syntax—three noun phrases in apposition—makes it impossible to clarify the reference, nor is it clear why there is a shift in voice from third to first person at this point.

One must conclude that, read as an "ontologically complete" poem, "Nostalgia" is something less than successful. The meaning of the narrative is not sharply focused, the images—many of which seem gratuitous—are not organized into a coherent structure, and the tone wavers uneasily between a detached third-person account of an event and the painfully personal involvement of an "I." Such irresolution is not characteristic of the poems in *Life Studies* (1959) or *For the Union Dead* (1964). If we wish to understand what problems Lowell faced in transforming the original Rimbaud text into "alive English," we must now turn to "Mémoire" itself.

One of Rimbaud's last poems, "Mémoire" * is extremely elliptical and condensed: it looks ahead to the technique of the *Illuminations*. Lowell's imitation seems to be based less on a close consideration of the text itself than on the narrowly biographical reading the poem has been given by certain critics. In an early study of Rimbaud, Marcel Coulon advanced the thesis that "Mémoire" deals with the poet's

* For the text of the poem, see the end of the chapter.

recollection of his father's desertion: "Nous avons ici la scène de rupture entre Frédéric et Vitalie. Scène motivée par opposition complète de vue au sujet des enfants." [11] This reading of "Mémoire" is still current: Wallace Fowlie admits that other readings are possible but agrees with Coulon that "the poem is on the theme of flight" and that the third section can only be read as a painful account of the desertion of Rimbaud *père*.[12] However, although the biographical reading continues to persist in some quarters, in the past decade commentators have convincingly demonstrated that, like "Larme" or "Bateau ivre," "Mémoire" is essentially a visionary poem, describing the process whereby the *voyant* transcends his normal, routine consciousness and attains, if only for a brief moment, a vision of perfect felicity.[13]

René Etiemble was the first to notice that on the literal level "le thème est la course d'une rivière qui reflête successivement des lumières et des bords differents." [14] Once it is understood that "Elle" does not refer to Madame Rimbaud —or, for that matter, to a succession of different women as Fowlie suggests [15]—but to the river itself, and that the successive images evoked by the poet-speaker are dependent upon the changing appearance of the river landscape according to the movements of the sun from morning until dusk, the difficulties of interpretation are considerably reduced. Let us therefore begin with a consideration of the literal meaning of the poem.

The poet's reverie begins with a vision of clear water ("L'eau claire"), but immediately an overwhelming brightness, like the dazzlement caused by the salt of childhood tears, blinds his eye. This blinding whiteness conjures up images of the white bodies of women assaulting the sun, and white silk banners embossed with lilies,[16] rustling beneath an old wall, once defended by a young maid. The series of fragmentary utterances in the first stanza culminate in the phrase "l'ébat des anges" in line 5. The river, seen in the white morning sunlight, suggests to the poet-speaker a world of wonderful, dazzling whiteness, a pure story-book world of the Middle Ages, replete with white banners bearing the *fleur de lis* and a young virgin, reminiscent of Joan of Arc, on the battlements. The play of sunlight on the river suggests to him the innocent joy of angels at play.

But with the word "Non" in line 5 there is a shift in mood. The dazzling whiteness gives way to the golden light of midday, and correspondingly the content of the poet's vision becomes less innocent, more sensual. The golden river is seen as a female presence, moving its arms "noirs et lourds, et frais surtout, d'herbe." The riverbanks, with their black earth and rich grass, are thus compared to the arms of the sinuously winding "courant d'or." These sexual connotations continue to operate in the next two lines: with the blue sky as an overarching canopy, the river sinks down into her bed, shadowed by the curtains formed by the hillside and the bridge above it. And now in section ii, the poet experiences a moment of total joy. As the sun rises to its full height "au midi prompt," the watery surface of the river reflects such golden light that it seems to extend its "bouillons limpides" over the whole meadow, filling the banks with pale, bottomless gold. In an animistic reversal, even the faded green dresses of the little girls, sitting on the riverbank, are transformed into weeping willows in whose branches unfettered little birds hop about. The river mirrors the sun so perfectly that it seems to have its own source of light within; indeed, the little marsh marigold ("le souci d'eau"), in color and shape like a gold coin or a warm, round eyelid, is now outshining that other sun, the "Sphère rose et chère" in the heavens. The apostrophe, "ta foi conjugale, ô l'Epouse!", suggests that the golden flower has become the emblem of the conjugal faith of the river bride; it symbolizes the marriage of river and sun.

But now in the third section the vision of a silky, golden

world breaks down, giving way to something quite different. Here if anywhere in the poem, Rimbaud seems to refer to his father's desertion of his mother ("Madame"). In her notes to the Garnier edition, however, Suzanne Bernard points out that "Lui" in line 20 may refer, quite simply, to the sun whose light, like a band of angels, suddenly disappears behind the mountain.[17] In this case, the "Madame" who stands too straight in the field and steps on the little white flower, represents the perverse human will that forces the sun to go away, that makes nature turn black. She is a kind of mythic Black Woman, the enemy of all that is spontaneous and fresh. In any case, the gold is now gone. The moment of joy has passed.

In section iv, the poet is thus overwhelmed by a sense of loss and defeat: the magical river with its thick young arms of pure grass and its gold of April moons has vanished and so has the "Joie / des chantiers riverains à l'abandon," the joy of being alone in abandoned boatyards where, on August nights, one could watch rotting things ("ces pourritures") come to life. Separated from her spouse the sun, the magically sensuous stream turns into a perfectly ordinary river, in whose murky waters one is not surprised to find an old dredger, laboring in his motionless boat. The gray surface of this river no longer reflects anything.

Having lost his vision, the poet awakens to find that he himself is the "vieux, dragueur," whose motionless boat is stuck in the mud of the river bottom. Like the frail little boat in the cold black puddle of "Bateau ivre," the "canot immobile" of line 34 metaphorically stands for the trapped self of the poet. His arms are too short to reach the yellow and blue flowers, the willows are dusty, and the reeds, no longer bathed in the rosy glow of the sun, have been devoured by the darkening night. The surface of the water has lost all shape or configuration: it is rimless ("sans bords"), amorphous, ill-defined. As night falls, only the mud in which the boat's chain is caught seems real. The self can no longer make contact with the source of joy, of life.

Despite difficulties of diction and syntax,[18] the formal design of "Mémoire" is beautifully articulated. Temporally, the structure of its imagery is very simple: the movement is from dawn to dusk, from light to darkness. But within this external temporal frame, images are related not temporally, spatially, or logically, but according to their symbolic overtones. This aspect of Rimbaud's poetry has been examined in a brilliant essay by Jean-Pierre Richard in *Poésie et Profondeur*. Although Richard does not discuss "Mémoire" except in passing, his description of Rimbaud's poetic cosmos is extremely helpful in clarifying the relationship of images in this particular poem.

For Rimbaud, Richard observes, the central myth is that of the flood—not the flood that descends from heaven to inundate the earth, but a deluge that comes from the earth itself with a powerful upward thrust, "un égouttement montant." "Le Paradis rimbaldien," according to Richard, "c'est . . . le monde humecté, la terre éponge. Et l'on comprend alors pourquoi Rimbaud est à ce point sensible à toutes les formes d'affleurement liquide, pourquoi il aime si particulièrement les substances—boues, mousses ou gazon—qui puissent s'imbiber de l'eau profonde et la transporter à travers elles jusqu'au jour. C'est la porosité qui permet l'éclosion." [19] For Rimbaud, the vision of eternity is thus prefigured in the moment in which the mysterious earth comes to life: flowers open their petals, blades of grass shoot up, and subterranean streams flood the marshy meadows.

It is fascinating to note that almost all the images whose recurrence Richard traces throughout Rimbaud's work are contained in one relatively short poem like "Mémoire": grass ("verdure fleurie," "ses bras . . . frais surtout, d'herbe," "Regret des bras épais et jeunes d'herbe pure!"); silk ("la soie, en foule et de lys pur"); little wild flowers ("le souci d'eau," "l'ombelle," "la jaune qui m'importune," "la bleue, amie à l'eau couleur de cendre," "Les roses des roseaux"); trees that grow in marshy soil ("les saules"); birds preparing for flight ("ou sautent les oiseaux sans brides"); the rippling surface of water ("l'humide carreau tend ses bouillons limpides! / L'eau meuble d'or pale et sans fond les couches prêtes"); the moist and fecund earth ("germer ces pourritures"); small round globes, such as tear drops ("larmes d'enfance"), coins ("Plus pure qu'un louis"), or round eyelids ("jaune et chaude paupière"); and finally one of Rimbaud's favorite images: molten gold ("le courant d'or en marche," "L'eau meuble d'or pale," "Or des lunes d'avril au coeur du saint lit").[20]

Rimbaud's flowers, drops of water, stones and white silks undergo amazing metamorphoses. "L'étude du lapidaire rimbaldien," Richard points out, "montre bien que sa geologie recouvre en fait une botanique, que la pierre represente pour lui un *fruit,* un vivant produit de la terre: comme dans la fleur il choisissait surtout de voir la floraison, il imagine dans la pierre les obscures operations d'une genèse." [21] So in "Mémoire" the gold marsh marigold imperceptibly becomes a gold coin or a golden drop of water. Everything merges in this world of underground deluge. The jet of life springs up from below: the phrase, "L'assaut au soleil des blancheurs des corps de femme," for example, suggests that a dazzling white substance is shooting upward to the heavens to hit the target of the sun.

Conversely, everything that negates the world of vision is dry, stiff, cold, and either black or colorless. The sensuously female river, with its bed, blue sky canopy, and thick grassy arms, is replaced by "Madame" who "se tient trop debout dans la prairie." The drab world of everyday life is characterized by "la nappe, sans reflets, sans source, grise," by "la poudre des saules," and by the "canot immobile," whose anchor is "tiré / Au fond de cet oeil d'eau sans bords,—à quelle boue"—a muddy substance that, unlike the "pourritures" of line 28, is so hard and dry that the chain cannot break loose.

"Mémoire" has, then, a rich thematic design in which one set of images (grass-flower-silk-mineral-moisture) is juxtaposed to another (mud-cold-blackness-surface without depth-immobility), and indeed these two sets of images reappear with enormously inventive variations throughout Rimbaud's poetry. The question that now arises, as we turn back to Lowell's "Nostalgia," is whether such a complex thematic design can be transferred from the parent text to a verse translation which is, by Lowell's own admission, "reckless with literal meaning" (*Imit*, xi). Can a poet, in other words, discard certain images, retain others, or invert their connotations at will and still produce a poem which, when read independently, has its own coherence and central design? Let us now summarize the ways in which Lowell has transformed his model.

(1) Lowell retains most of Rimbaud's nature images—the "gold stream," "white lilies on white silk," "marsh marigolds," and so forth—but these images are not closely related to one another or to a central myth of the flood as they are in "Mémoire." On the contrary, their symbolic value seems to be somewhat arbitrarily assigned. When, for example, the first line of "Mémoire": "L'eau claire; comme le sel des larmes d'enfance" becomes "The sucking river was the child's salt tears," the connotations of the salty tear drops are exactly reversed. The same process occurs in the second line: "His eyes were blinded by white walls" has unpleasant connotations of restriction and obstruction totally absent from "L'assaut au soleil des blancheurs des corps de femme." In the third line, Lowell seems to retain Rimbaud's meaning: "White lilies on white silk," but since the silk is that of the *Tricouleur*, the import of the image is not certain. In the

second stanza, we may note the same irresolution. "Wings of an angel!" retains the general meaning of "l'ébat des anges," and Lowell's gold stream "breathing the underwater amber" is akin to Rimbaud's "courant d'or en marche." But in lines 7–8, Lowell translates "Elle" as "His mother," and so the sensuous river, languidly reclining in its bed of love, becomes the frigid woman who rejects the blue sky and "begged the arched bridge and the hills for shade."

This sudden switch suggests that Lowell's imitation is neither fish nor fowl; it is at once too free a translation and not free enough. For if the white light suggests the wings of angels and the river is a lovely golden stream, why does Lowell invert the meaning of lines 7–8? We can detect this uncomfortable shifting of ground throughout "Nostalgia," and although it would be tedious to cite all instances, let me mention just a few others. In lines 11–12, Rimbaud's faded green dresses which animistically become lovely willow trees full of birds, are given the opposite meaning in "Nostalgia"; "the sisters' faded grass-bruised pinafores / hung like willows." Lowell's image is depressing: the little girls are seen as part of the mother's lifeless ambiance. Again, the moment of felicity in Stanza IV of "Mémoire" is replaced in "Nostalgia" by images of oppressive, steamy noonday heat, even though the apostrophe to the Bride and the reference to the marigold are oddly retained. The most dramatic change comes in the first stanza of section iv: the reference to arms, grass, and the gold of April moons is retained, but the arms of the river become the hairy arms of the "lost man," and the "holy April moonlight" now refers to the lost happiness of the mother. Rimbaud's abandoned boatyards, those mysterious places where rotting things germinate and where the poet's imagination can conjure up images of voyage and adventure, become in Lowell's poem lumberyards which pollute the marsh with blocks and sawdust. In this stanza, much of Rim-

baud's diction and phrasing is retained, but the meaning
that emerges is the opposite of Rimbaud's.

We can now understand why "Nostalgia" seems so confusing when it is read as an independent poem. In retaining
some of Rimbaud's nature images and transforming or discarding others, Lowell destroys a carefully conceived imagistic design *without replacing it with anything else.* Ironically,
he has not been "reckless" enough "with literal meaning." If
his poem is meant to convey the frustrations of repressed
childhood—as I think it is—then the images of white silk,
gold amber, and wings of an angel have no relevance and
should have been dropped altogether.

(2) Rimbaud's imagery is purposely vague, dreamlike, hallucinatory. He refers to "pucelle" rather than to Joan of Arc,
to "oriflammes" rather than to a particular flag, because he
wants to describe a transcendent reality which can be at least
partially apprehended through these references to maidens
and white silk flags. What Lowell has done in "Nostalgia" is
to *psychologize* Rimbaud's imagery, to make it more concrete, more specific—and hence much narrower in scope.
Thus, in the lines referred to above, Rimbaud's vision of
white radiance gives way to Lowell's ironic commentary on
the place of the *Tricouleur* in Joan of Arc's France.

In making Rimbaud's images more explicit, Lowell tends
to explain them away. For example, Rimbaud's "foulant
l'ombelle: trop fière pour elle," suggests that, although she is
destructive, "Madame" is also rather pathetic in her strange
envy of a little white flower. But Lowell's "trampled on the
weeds" gives a one-dimensional image of a neurotic person
exerting her will. Similarly, whereas in "Mémoire," the children, who are never specified, are pictured "lisant dans la
verdure fleurie / leur livre de maroquin rouge," in "Nostalgia," the children explicitly become Rimbaud's sisters; the
"verdure fleurie"—Rimbaud's magic green carpet—becomes

the "heraldic green," and the red morocco book is designated as the Missal. Rimbaud's image suggests that to read a book on a sunny day is an act of irreverence to "la verdure fleurie." Lowell's version, on the other hand, implies that Rimbaud's sisters are the victims of their mother's misguided zeal: they are forced to keep their heads in their prayer books. This pointed autobiographical reference is out of keeping with certain other passages: if, like the Vitalie Rimbaud of real life, the mother is a religious fanatic, why does she long for the "holy April moonlight" and the "hairy arms" of her "lost man" in the fourth section?

Here again one must conclude that Lowell's imitation falls between two stools. The poet might have recast "Mémoire" in the mold of *Life Studies,* inventing an autobiographical narrative in which the childhood sufferings of the representative poet would be presented with the mixture of sympathy and irony found in a poem such as "Grandparents," or he might have adhered more closely to his model. As it stands, however, "Nostalgia" is neither a poem of visionary quest nor a consistent psychological narrative.

(3) This ambivalence is reflected even in the syntax of "Nostalgia." With respect to stanza form and meter, Lowell follows his model fairly closely.[22] But his departure from Rimbaud's typical syntactic patterns is particularly revealing. In "Mémoire," the speaker's emotion is maintained in a continuous present. The sentence structure is consistently paratactic: short, fragmentary noun phrases with heavy adjectival modification alternate with declarative sentences loosely strung together without temporal or causal connectives. The mode, as the five interjections and nine exclamation points suggest, is exclamatory, incantatory, and invocative; the alexandrine all but breaks down in certain places (for example, lines 5, 14, 21) as the speaker pieces together his fragmentary vision. Viewed as a whole, the poem reenacts the process whereby the memory calls up successive images,

often seemingly disconnected. The images pass, one by one, across the speaker's field of vision with an almost cinematic vividness and immediacy.

Lowell changes the tense of Rimbaud's poem from present to past: lyric utterance becomes sequential narrative. "Mémoire"—that abstract word—becomes the "Nostalgia" *for* something. Rimbaud's exclamatory noun phrases—for example, "L'assaut au soleil des blancheurs des corps de femme"—become declarative sentences: "His eyes were blinded by white walls." But despite the matter-of-factness of such sentences as "The sucking river was the child's salt tears," Lowell has a hard time in making a "story" out of Rimbaud's elusive images. The expectations raised by a sentence like "Then the walled surface swam with bubbles" are never fulfilled. "*Then* what happened?" the reader wonders. One senses that Lowell himself realized that the story was not taking shape, for he provides the missing scenario in the parenthetical note that acts as epigraph.

The distinctions I have been making suggest that Lowell and Rimbaud are in fact very different poetic sensibilities. Rimbaud's poetry is what Northrop Frye has called the "poetry of process"; [23] his is an oracular mode in which the "I" is concerned to utter rather than to address and speaks in a state of rapt self-communion. Identifying animistically with the processes of nature, he himself becomes the river with the heavy arms of grass, or the golden marigold whose light rivals that of the sun. Lowell, in contrast, has a historical rather than a visionary imagination. At his best he is a Chekhovian realist, presenting an ironically distanced and lovingly particularized image of himself—an image at once concrete and universal in its implications. For Rimbaud, there is only the present with its occasional intimations of the perfect world of the future; for Lowell, the present is the natural culmination of all that has gone before, and it can only be understood in the light of the past. In his autobiographical poems, Lowell makes the past live; in Rimbaud's poetry there is almost always a blurred sense of events, and of temporal and spatial relationships. Rimbaud's nature imagery is totally alien to Lowell, who is at home in the blighted urban landscape of the Boston Common or on the banks of the Hudson River, whose waters are filled with tin cans and waste paper rather than with golden marigolds or white silk.

As a translation, "Nostalgia" is open to attack because of its lack of fidelity to the parent text: the reader without French who wants as close an approximation as possible to Rimbaud's poem will obviously have to go elsewhere. As an original poem, on the other hand, "Nostalgia" is too dependent on another text; it is, paradoxically, too much of a translation. Restricted by the actual imagery and tone of Rimbaud, Lowell cannot break loose enough to find his own tone.

One might of course argue that Lowell is more successful an "imitator" when he adapts poems by writers whose style is closer to his own—for example, Montale or Baudelaire. Indeed, both D. S. Carne-Ross and Ben Belitt make good cases for the success of Lowell's renderings of Montale.[24] Nevertheless, even Belitt concludes from his analysis of "Dora Markus" that "it is a *translated* and not an 'imitated' poem. Every sequence of Montale's thinking has been retained intact, every image has been confronted, for the most part, in its own context." "Dora Markus" is, in other words, a generally faithful translation.

Lowell's theory of "imitation" thus remains problematic. Every major poet inhabits his own poetic universe; his images, verb tenses, and sentence structure reflect a way of looking at experience. But when a second poet takes over an existing structure, retaining some items, transforming others, and discarding those that do not suit him, the poetic structure breaks down. Simply put, grass does not mean to

Lowell what it meant to Rimbaud: Lowell's grass is just another item in a dingy, dusty landscape. In breaking up the grass-gold-water-flower cluster, he thus tampers with the internal poetic relationships of "Mémoire." One wonders, then, whether even as fine a poet as Lowell can write an "original sequence" that is "based on the work of 18 European poets." Such hybrid translation is hardly "immoral"—after all, Lowell always acknowledges his source and challenges us to go back to the original—but neither does it produce poems whose artistry is wholly satisfying.

Nostalgia

(An autobiographical poem: Rimbaud remembers the small boy in a rowboat under the old walls of Charleville. His mother and sisters are on the bank. His father has just deserted them.)

I

The sucking river was the child's salt tears.
His eyes were blinded by white walls; the girls
white lilies on white silk! The *Tricouleur*
hung from the walls restored by Joan of Arc—

wings of an angel! No, the gold stream slid,   5
breathing the underwater amber of its reeds . . .
His mother had the blue sky for parasol,
yet begged the arched bridge and the hills for shade.

II

Then the walled surface swam with bubbles;
cloth of gold coverings piled the riverbed;   10
the sisters' faded grass-bruised pinafores
hung like willows; birds stepped from twig to twig.

Through noon, the river's spotted mirror steamed
off to the bare sky's perfect, burning sphere—
Oh Bride, your faith was purer than gold coins,   15
marsh marigolds my hot and burning eyelid . . .

III

The mother stood too stiffly in the field,
beclouded with the field-hands' shirts. She twirled
her parasol, and trampled on the weeds.
The sisters sat on the heraldic green,   20

and stared at red Morocco Missals, while
his father walked beyond the mountain, like
a thousand angels, parting on the road.
She, cold and black, flew. Rushed after her lost man!

IV

Nostalgia for his hairy arms—the grass   25
green in the holy April moonlight! Joy!
The riverbank's abandoned lumberyards
still fertilized the marsh with blocks and sawdust.

She wept below the parapet. The breath
of the dry poplars was the wind's alone;   30
the water had no bottom and no source;
a man in mud-caked hip-boots poled a barge.

V

The dull eye drove the water out of reach—
still boat, oh too short arms! I could not touch
one or the other flower—the yellow burned me,   35
the cool blue was the ash-gray water's friend.

The reeds had eaten up the roses long ago;
each wing-beat shook the willows' silver dust.
My boat stuck fast; its anchor dug for bottom;
the lidless eye, still water, filled with mud.   40

Mémoire [25]

by Arthur Rimbaud

I

L'eau claire; comme le sel des larmes d'enfance,
L'assaut au soleil des blancheurs des corps de femme;

la soie, en foule et des lys pur, des oriflammes
sous les murs dont quelque pucelle eut la défense;

l'ébat des anges;—Non . . . le courant d'or en marche,   5
meut ses bras, noirs et lourds, et frais surtout, d'herbe. Elle
sombre, ayant le Ciel bleu pour ciel-de-lit, appelle
pour rideaux l'ombre de la colline et de l'arche.

II

Eh! l'humide carreau tend ses bouillons limpides!
L'eau meuble d'or pâle et sans fond les couches prêtes;   10
Les robes vertes et deteintes des fillettes
font les saules, d'où sautent les oiseaux sans brides.

Plus pure qu'un louis, jaune et chaude paupière
le souci d'eau—ta foi conjugale, ô l'Epouse!—
au midi prompt, de son terne miror, jalouse   15
au ciel gris de chaleur la Sphère rose et chère.

III

Madame se tient trop debout dans la prairie
prochaine où neigent les fils du travail; l'ombrelle
aux doigts; foulant l'ombelle; trop fière pour elle;
des enfants lisant dans la verdure fleurie   20

leur livre de maroquin rouge! Hélas! Lui, comme
mille anges blancs qui se séparent sur la route,
s'éloigne par delà la montagne! Elle, toute
froide, et noire, court! apres le départ de l'homme!

IV

Regret des bras épais et jeunes d'herbe pure!   25
Or des lunes d'avril au coeur du saint lit! Joie
des chantiers riverains à l'abandon, en proie
aux soirs d'août qui faisaient germer ces pourritures.

Qu'elle pleure à présent sous les remparts! l'haleine
des peupliers d'en haut est pour la seule brise.   30
Puis, c'est la nappe, sans reflets, sans source, grise:
un vieux, drageur, dans sa barque immobile, peine.

V

Jouet de cet oeil d'eau morne, je n'y puis prendre,
o canot immobile! oh! bras trop courts! ni l'une
ni l'autre fleur: ni la la jaune qui m'importune   35
la; ni la bleue, amie à l'eau couleur de cendre.

A! la poudre des saules qu'une aile secoue!
Les roses des roseaux dés longtemps dévoreés!
Au fond de cet oeil d'eau sans bords,—à quelle boue?   40

Mémoire

translated by Wallace Fowlie

I

Clear water; like the salt of childhood tears;
The assault on the sun by the whiteness of women's bodies;
the silk of banners, in masses and of pure lilies,
under the walls a maid once defended.

The play of angels—No . . . the golden current on its way   5
moves its arms, black and heavy, and above all cool, with
    grass. She
dark, having the blue sky as a canopy, calls up
for curtains the shadow of the hill and the arch.

II

Ah! the wet surface extends its clear broth!
The water fills the prepared beds with pale bottomless gold.   10
The green faded dresses of girls
make willows out of which hop unbridled birds.

Purer than a louis, a yellow and warm eyelid:
the marsh marigold—your conjugal faith, O Spouse—
At prompt noon, from its dim mirror, vies   15
with the dear rose Sphere in the sky grey with heat.

III

Madame stands too straight in the field
nearby where the filaments from the (harvest) work snow
    down; the parasol
in her fingers; stepping on the white flower, too proud for
    her;
children reading in the flowering grass   20

their book of red morocco. Alas, he, like
a thousand white angels separating on the road,
goes off beyond the mountain! She, all
cold and dark, runs! after the departing man!

IV

Longings for the thick young arms of pure grass!   25
Gold of April moons in the heart of the holy bed; joy
of abandoned boatyards, a prey
to August nights which made rotting things germinate!

Let her weep now under the ramparts! the breath
of the poplars above is the only breeze.   30
After, there is the surface, without reflection, without
    springs, gray:
an old dredger, in his motionless boat, labors.

V

Toy of this sad eye of water, I cannot pluck,
O motionless boat! O arms too short, either this
Or the other flower: neither the yellow one which bothers me   35
There, nor the friendly blue one in the ash-colored water.

Ah! dust of the willows shaken by a wing!
The roses of the reeds devoured long ago!
My boat still stationary, and its chain caught
In the bottom of this rimless eye of water—in what mud?   40

Chapter Three

The Confessional Mode:
Romanticism and Realism

To *sound* personal is the point.
James Merrill

In exploring the contours of the Lowell landscape, my emphasis has necessarily been on the thematic function of Lowell's imagery. I wish now to turn to a related topic: the structural relationships of Lowell's images within the individual poem. Specifically, I want to examine the structures found in Lowell's confessional poetry, the poetry inaugurated in 1959 by *Life Studies,* which had such a profound influence on the lyric poetry of the sixties.

As long ago as 1925, Boris Tomashevsky, a leading Russian formalist critic, observed that the "autobiographical poem" is one that mythologizes the poet's life in accordance with the conventions of his time. It relates not what has occurred but what should have occurred, presenting an idealized image of the poet as representative of his literary school.[1] James Merrill made the same point with reference to the so-called confessional poems in his *Nights and Days* (1967): "Confessional Poetry . . . is a literary convention like any other, the problem being to make it *sound* as if it were true." Whether or not the poet is presenting the actual facts of his experience is irrelevant, but he must give the "illusion of a True Confession."[2] "There's a good deal of tinkering with fact," Lowell said of *Life Studies* in the *Paris Review* interview, but of course "the reader was to believe he was getting the *real* Robert Lowell."[3]

These reminders of the role convention plays in even autobiographical poetry are salutary at a time when the confessional poem—surely our predominant lyric genre today—is consistently treated by critics as *confession* rather than as *poetry*. When M. L. Rosenthal, in his seminal study of postwar poetry, defines the confessional poem as one in which "the private life of the poet himself, especially under stress of psychological crisis, becomes a major theme," [4] he is telling us something about the typical subject matter of Robert Lowell or Allen Ginsberg or Anne Sexton, but this and similar definitions give us no way of distinguishing between, say, Anne Sexton's frequently maudlin revelations of her reactions to menstruation or masturbation and a poem like Lowell's "Skunk Hour"—generally considered one of the major poems of the last decade.[5]

Again, when critics argue, as Roger Bowen has done,[6] that *Life Studies* functioned mainly as a "personal catharsis" for the poet, and that, once Lowell had been liberated from the "personal neurosis" and the "obsessive involvement with personal history" which characterize these confessional poems, he was psychologically ready to move on to a more "responsible" and more "public" poetry, I suspect that the nature of the confessional poem as a literary genre has been completely misunderstood. The publication of *Notebook 1967–68* must in fact have come as a great surprise to critics of Bowen's persuasion, for here, ten years after *Life Studies,* were poems about Lowell's precise sensations during the Pentagon March of 1967, his idyllic romance during a brief stay at Harvard, his ambivalent feelings toward Allen Tate and Randall Jarrell, and his reactions to too much liquor. Read as a whole, *Notebook 1967–68* is, despite Lowell's disclaimer in the "Afterthought," [7] an autobiographical sequence in which one year in the life of Robert Lowell is recaptured. Although the stanza form—the blank verse sonnet —of *Notebook* is new, the mode of the poems is still that of *Life Studies.*

How does a poet like Lowell "mythologize" his personal life? What are the conventions that govern the structure of his poems, and conversely, what conventions does he reject? These are the questions I shall try to answer in this chapter. My text is one of the best-known poems in the final section of *Life Studies,* "Man and Wife":

Tamed by *Miltown,* we lie on Mother's bed;
the rising sun in war paint dyes us red;
in broad daylight her gilded bed-posts shine,
abandoned, almost Dionysian.
At last the trees are green on Marlborough Street,
blossoms on our magnolia ignite
the morning with their murderous five days' white.
All night I've held your hand,
as if you had
a fourth time faced the kingdom of the mad—
its hackneyed speech, its homicidal eye—
and dragged me home alive. . . . Oh my *Petite,*
clearest of all God's creatures, still all air and nerve:
you were in your twenties, and I,
once hand on glass
and heart in mouth,
outdrank the Rahvs in the heat
of Greenwich Village, fainting at your feet—
too boiled and shy
and poker-faced to make a pass,
while the shrill verve
of your invective scorched the traditional South.

Now twelve years later, you turn your back.
Sleepless, you hold
your pillow to your hollows like a child;
your old-fashioned tirade—
loving, rapid, merciless—
breaks like the Atlantic Ocean on my head.   [*LS,* 87]

I suppose that the most obvious thing to say about this poem is that it marks a return to the romantic mode in which the "I," clearly designated as the poet himself, undergoes a highly personal experience. Whatever else "Man and Wife" is like, it surely represents a reaction against Eliot's dictum that poetry is not the turning loose of emotion but an escape from emotion; it is a reaction against the autonomous, "impersonal" symbolist mode of Eliot, Pound, Stevens, the early Auden, and of the Robert Lowell of *Lord Weary's Castle*—the mode that dominated the first half of our century. Lowell himself has said that when he wrote *Life Studies,* he wanted to get away from the doctrine that poetry is first of all a craft. "Any number of people are guilty of writing a complicated poem that has a certain amount of symbolism in it and really difficult meaning, a wonderful poem to teach. Then you unwind it and you feel that the intelligence, the experience, whatever goes into it, is skin deep." [8] More explicitly, W. D. Snodgrass has said in a panel discussion, "I read *The Waste Land* if somebody tells me to but I never tell myself to. Similarly with Pound, I am much attracted to his early work but I find that as he goes on he becomes less and less a poet and more and more a kind of flash card machine." As for Stevens, his whole middle period is "a desert of philosophy." Interestingly, the only early twentieth-century poet exempt from these charges is Yeats. He was, Snodgrass believes, "the last and certainly the finest symbolist in English. Yet in some very essential sense he never gave in to it." He could not submit to any "system of ideas" because he was essentially "talking about his own feelings." [9] Yeats is, in other words, a romantic and therefore, unlike Eliot and Pound, he is acceptable to a confessional poet of the mid-sixties.

M. H. Abrams defines the structure of what he calls "the greater Romantic lyric" as follows:

[It presents] a determinate speaker in a particularized, and usually a localized, outdoor setting, whom we overhear as he carries on, in a fluent vernacular which rises easily to a more formal speech, a sustained colloquy, sometimes with himself or with the outer scene, but more frequently with a silent human auditor, present or absent. The speaker begins with a description of the landscape; an aspect or change of aspect in the landscape evokes a varied but integral process of memory, thought, anticipation, and feeling which remains closely involved with the outer scene. In the course of this meditation the lyric speaker achieves an insight, faces up to a tragic loss, comes to a moral decision, or resolves an emotional problem. Often the poem rounds upon itself to end where it began, at the outer scene, but with an altered mood and deepened understanding which is the result of the intervening meditation.[10]

This definition is generally applicable to the structure of "Man and Wife," even though the bedroom has replaced the outdoor setting of romantic poetry. Lowell's poem does have a determinate speaker—the poet himself—in a specific setting at a particular moment in time, who carries on a colloquy with a silent human auditor—his wife. Again, the poet does use a "fluent vernacular" ("All night I've held your hand") which "rises easily to a more formal speech" as in "Oh my *Petite,* / clearest of all God's creatures." The poem begins in the present: husband and wife face the beginning of another day not after a happy night of love, but after sleepless hours of argument, hysteria, and anxiety, made bearable only by tranquillizers. As the poet contemplates the scene, he recalls the very different night of their first meeting. The memory of his former enthusiastic and romantic self enables the poet to face the present with some return to equanimity: wryly he capitulates to his wife's "old-fashioned tirade" which "breaks like the Atlantic" on his head. The poem thus "rounds upon itself"; it moves in a circle from present to past and back to the present, imitating the structure of the poet's meditation as he struggles toward self-understanding.

Generically, then, "Man and Wife" can be placed in the

romantic tradition, and yet even a cursory reading of the poem suggests that it is, in fact, quite unlike "Resolution and Independence" or "Frost at Midnight" or "Ode to a Nightingale." One notices immediately the factual documentation quite alien to the romantics: the allusions to *Miltown*, to Marlborough Street, to the Rahvs of Greenwich Village, as well as the peculiar insistence on numerical accuracy: "five days' white," "a fourth time," "you were in your twenties," "twelve years later." Conversely, "Man and Wife" does not have the dense web of symbolic implication that characterizes romantic and symbolist poetry. The magnolia tree of line 6, for example, unlike the "great-rooted blossomer" of Yeats's "Among School Children" or the "green laurel" of his "Prayer for my Daugher," is not a central symbol around which the whole poem is built. It would have no place, for example, in the rich catalogue of tree images discussed by Frank Kermode in *Romantic Image*.[11] One finds it difficult, moreover, to discern what relates one line or one image to the next in "Man and Wife." Why, for example, does the poem begin with the image of the tranquillized couple reclining on "Mother's bed"—an image rich with latent meanings about the failure of this particular marriage —and then suddenly switch to the optical effect created when bright sunlight shines on bed-posts? Although the syntax is perfectly straightforward—a sequence of simple declarative sentences—the poet's meditation is not sustained. It focuses first on one object and then on another without explicit connection.

How, then, can we characterize the technique of "Man and Wife"? Lowell himself gives us an important hint when, in the *Paris Review* interview, he explains why he rejected the technically sophisticated poetry of his contemporaries, a poetry exhibiting "tremendous skill" but "divorced from culture somehow." "Prose," Lowell argues, "is in many ways better off than poetry. It's quite hard to think of a young poet who has the vitality, say, of Salinger or Saul Bellow. . . . Some of this Alexandrian poetry is very brilliant. . . . But I thought it was getting increasingly stifling. I couldn't get my experience into tight metrical forms." [12]

"Almost the whole problem of writing poetry," Lowell insists, "is to bring it back to what you really feel." The "ideal modern form" for capturing "personal vibrance" is the novel. "Maybe Tolstoy would be the perfect example—his work is imagistic, it deals with all experience, and there seems to be no conflict of the form and content. So one thing is to get into poetry that kind of human richness in rather simple descriptive language." [13] In a later discussion of *Life Studies* Lowell made this point even more emphatic: "I felt that the best style for poetry was none of the many poetic styles in English, but something like the prose of Chekhov or Flaubert." [14]

In *Life Studies,* one concludes, Lowell is trying to fuse the romantic mode, which projects the poet's "I" in the act of self-discovery, and the Tolstoyan or Chekhovian mode, usually called realism. I would posit that it is his superb manipulation of the realistic convention, rather than the titillating confessional content, that is responsible for the so-called breakthrough of *Life Studies* and that distinguishes Lowell's confessional poetry from the work of his less accomplished disciples. [15]

Realism is one of the most difficult terms to define, as René Wellek's and Harry Levin's comprehensive discussions of the term in literary scholarship make clear. [16] Tolstoyan realism is perhaps best defined in an excellent essay on *Anna Karenina* by Robert Louis Jackson: "The principle of realism guilding Tolstoy . . . is one which Chekhov will develop to the highest point of perfection; the view that our casual everyday appearance, behavior, conversation—in short, our everyday 'character' and confrontations—contain, reflect, anticipate the larger shape of our destiny." Tolstoy's genius is "to maintain a primary focus upon the 'natural' movement of surface action . . . while at the same time revealing in this seemingly routine material the texture of a dynamic reality, rapidly acquiring design and shape." [17]

But how does the realistic writer organize "seemingly routine material" so that it will reveal the "texture of a dynamic reality"? It was Roman Jakobson, I believe, who first associated realism with metonymy as a stylistic device. Any verbal discourse, Jakobson argues, has two possible poles of semantic connection between words or word groups: relations of similarity or of contiguity. If, for example, the stimulus *hut* produces the response *poor little house,* the relationship is one of semantic similarity, since the second term can obviously be substituted for the first. If, on the other hand, the response to the stimulus *hut* is *poverty,* the link is one of contiguity, the focus shifting from one term to a closely related one.[18]

In literature, Jakobson observes, the figures of semantic similarity are simile and metaphor, whereas contiguity produces the figures traditionally known as metonymy and synecdoche. "The primacy of the metaphoric process in the literary schools of romanticism and symbolism has been repeatedly acknowledged," writes Jakobson, "but it is still insufficiently realized that it is the predominance of metonymy which underlies and actually predetermines the so-called 'realist' trend. Following the path of contiguous relations, the realistic author metonymically digresses from the plot to the atmosphere and from the characters to the setting in space and time." [19] In Pasternak's early prose, for example, there is a "tendency to substitute the 'action' for the 'actor,' and the 'setting' for the 'action,' to resolve the image of the hero into . . . a series of objectified states of mind or of surrounding objects." [20]

In *Theory of Literature,* René Wellek and Austin Warren seem to echo Jakobson when they say that "metonymy and metaphor may be the characterizing structures of two poetic types—poetry of association by contiguity, of movement within a single world of discourse, and poetry of association by comparison, joining a plurality of worlds." [21] But most critics have been extremely reluctant to follow this lead, no doubt because their own orientation is toward symbolism and romanticism. Jerome Mazzaro, for example, has complained that "the most serious defect" of Lowell's confessional poetry is "the poet's inability to rise above simplified diction and imagery to a comment on life"; [22] he takes for granted that the dense symbolic mode of "The Quaker Graveyard in Nantucket," with its allusions to *Genesis, Revelation,* and *Moby Dick,* is somehow superior.[23]

Yet metonymic structure is far from artless. Before examining this technique in Lowell's poetry, it may be helpful to show how metonymy works in a realist novel like *Anna Karenina.* In chapter 30 of Part I, when Anna's train pulls into Petersburg after her fateful interview with Vronsky, she suddenly becomes aware of her husband, waiting on the station platform. " 'Oh mercy! Why do his ears look like that?' she thought, looking at his frigid and imposing figure, and especially at the ears that struck her at the moment as propping up the brim of his round hat." [24] Here the physical attribute —the protruding ears—metonymically stand for the whole man. To Anna, who has never really "seen" her husband before, he instantaneously becomes ridiculous and physically repulsive. That night, when she and her husband are about to go to bed, the same thought recurs: " 'But why is it his ears stick out so strangely?' " Notice that this is not an objective portrait of Karenin. Vronsky, seeing the husband of the woman he loves from the same train, notices not his ears but his "rather prominent spine"—a spine whose stiffness and inflexibility he will have much occasion to fear.[25]

My second example is a metonymic shift from actor to setting. On the first evening of Anna's return to Petersburg,

Karenin comes home from an important meeting at four o'clock, and as usual various functionaries are to dine with him and Anna. "Precisely at five o'clock, before the bronze Peter the First clock had struck the fifth stroke, Alexey Alexandrovitch came in, wearing a white tie and evening coat with two stars, as he had to go out directly after dinner." [26] Tolstoy links Karenin to one particular object in the room because he and that object are in fact identical: Karenin's whole life is dictated by considerations of punctuality and the proper use of clock time. Moreover, he plays the role of diplomat in the grand tradition of Peter the First. Finally, he himself is a "bronze" object, for in Anna's view he is quite incapable of feeling; she thinks of him as a "spiteful machine." [27]

Another typically Tolstoyan metonymic transfer is that from actor to action. At the beginning of chapter 24 in Part II, Vronsky leaves Anna to go to the races. She has just told him that she is pregnant with his child and they have agreed that now their liaison must come out into the open. "When Vronsky looked at his watch on the Karenins' balcony, he was so greatly agitated and lost in his thoughts that he saw the figures on the watch's face but could not take in what time it was." [28] Tolstoy does not describe Vronsky's emotional turmoil; he shows his peculiar failure to perform a routine act: looking at one's watch to tell the time. The brief image succinctly dramatizes his extreme agitation, but it also tells us something fundamental about Vronsky: caught up in the particulars of experience, he fails to discern the underlying pattern. He adores Anna but cannot understand what their relationship means to her or where it will lead. He looks at her but cannot tell the time.

Let us now return to our original text: Lowell's "Man and Wife." In this intensely personal poem, Lowell dramatizes the strains and stresses of his twelve-year-old marriage to Elizabeth Hardwick, a marriage in which, the poem implies, sexual passion has gradually given way to mutual psychological dependency. The poet's self is clearly at the center, but there is little direct expression of the complex feeling—a mixture of devotion and ironic detachment—that the poet has for his wife. Rather, the poem is organized around a metonymic network of images: the speaker is characterized by his environment while his wife is known only by her speech habits ("the shrill verve / of your invective," "your old-fashioned tirade—loving, rapid, merciless") and by certain physical gestures ("you turn your back," "you hold / your pillow to your hollows").

Although the mode of "Man and Wife" is essentially realistic, there are a number of local metaphors. The "rising sun" of line 2 becomes, in the diseased imagination of the poet who fears passion and vitality, an Indian savage in "war paint" who "dyes us red," the pun on "dyes" intensifying the death-in-life existence of the couple. Paradoxically, from the poet's point of view only inert objects receive the sun's life-giving warmth: the "gilded bed-posts" of line 3, which evidently have an antique floral motif, are seen as thyrsi, the phallic staffs carried by the Bacchantes in their rites honoring Dionysus. The magnolia blossoms, further reminders that April is the cruelest month, are murderous creatures who set the morning air on fire. And finally, the tirade of the poet's wife bombards his ear like an ocean wave breaking against a rock.

But the condition which causes the poet to see the sun as a feared savage and the white magnolia blossoms as "murderous" is defined by a larger metonymic sequence of alliterating nouns: "*M*iltown"—"*M*other's bed"—"*M*arlborough Street"—"our *m*agnolia." The first line of the poem looks casual and matter-of-fact until certain connections become apparent. The reference to *Miltown,* the first and most famous of the tranquillizers that came on the market in the fifties, rather than to, say, Equanil or Valium, is not coincidental.

For one thing, the liquids and nasals ("Tamed by *Miltown*, we *l*ie on *M*other's bed") point up the speaker's torpor and lassitude, but, more important, the name *Miltown* metonymically suggests such terms as *Mill town, mill stone,* and *small town*. The poet's state of anxiety is thus immediately seen as somehow representative of a larger American dilemma, of a crisis that occurs in Small Town or Any Town, U.S.A. The image of neurotic fracture is intensified in the second half of the line: the nuptial bed has been replaced by "Mother's bed"; her shadow, as it were, lies between husband and wife. In lines 8–12, moreover, it becomes clear that the poet's wife must act the role of mother to him; for the "fourth time" she has had to hold his hand and drag him "home alive."

The reference to Marlborough Street in line 5 introduces a new dimension: the poet's Beacon Hill background. "Hardly passionate Marlborough Street," as Lowell, paraphrasing Henry James, calls it in "Memories of West Street and Lepke," is the prototype of puritan, snobbish Back Bay Boston. In this environment, the poem suggests, the communion of marriage will forever be denied; the trees, even though they can be owned like "our magnolia," turn green too late. The metonymic sequence *Miltown—Mother's bed —Marlborough Street—our magnolia* thus establishes the nature of the poet's milieu: his is a tradition which is deadening. The economy of the seven-line portrait is striking; the word "abandoned," for example, is charged with meaning: it refers both to the "Dionysian" abandon that is denied to the tranquillized couple, and to the ironic fact that, although Mother has indeed "abandoned" her bed because, as we know from the preceding poems, she is dead, her ghost continues to haunt it.

In the second section (lines 8–22), the poet addresses his wife directly. The phrase "Oh my *Petite,* / clearest of all God's creatures, still all air and nerve" sounds mawkish when detached from the poem, but within the context it defines the speaker's wish to let his wife know that he still admires and loves her even if his love is impotent and destructive. Although she must act the role of Mother to him, he wants to think of her as his *"Petite."* And now he recalls the night, so different from this "homicidal" one, when he first met her. Again the focus is on setting rather than on emotion. The scene is diametrically opposed to that of Marlborough Street: it is the noisy, hot, alcoholic, left-wing Greenwich Village of Philip Rahv, the editor of *Partisan Review*. The poet wryly recalls his former self, "hand on glass / and heart in mouth," trying to outdrink the Rahvs and "fainting" at the feet of his future wife, the Southern-born lady intellectual whose "shrill invective" denounced the traditionalism of the Old South.

Past and present are related by an interesting shift in fire imagery. In the opening tableau, the fire is always outside the poet's self: only the bed-posts and the magnolia blossoms are capable of burning. But during their first meeting, the lovers had fire within themselves: in "the *heat* of Greenwich Village," the poet was "too *boiled* and shy / and poker-faced to make a pass," while his beloved's "invective *scorched* the traditional South."

The turn in the final section is quietly ironic: "Now twelve years later, you turn your back." Husband and wife no longer even try to touch. "Sleepless," she holds not him but her pillow to the "hollows" of her unsatisfied body. As in the past, rhetoric is her weapon, but whereas at the Rahvs the attack was good-humored and academic, now on "Mother's bed" life itself is at stake. But this is not to say that the poem is wholly pessimistic. The first water image in the poem—the image of the ocean wave breaking against the speaker's head—marks a turning point. The life-giving water rouses the poet from his *Miltown*-induced lethargy, a lethargy in which he envies the thyrsus-like bed-post, and brings him back to reality.

"Man and Wife" is a highly condensed presentation of a complex personal drama: the movement from a tranquillized present in which life itself is feared and denied, to the memory of a romanticized bohemian past, and back to the present with its open-eyed realization that marriage is torture but also salvation. That the poem has been accused of being too "prosaic" is ironic, for it is intentionally prosaic in a special sense of the word.[29] Unlike, say, Donne's lovers in "The Canonization," Lowell's are not compared to anything; their plight is dramatized in terms of selected, patterned detail. The repeated references to numbers, for example, help to establish the reliability of the speaker as witness: he knows that magnolia blossoms turn brown after five days; he recalls that he has had four bouts with mental illness; he contrasts the image of his wife when she was in her twenties with what she has become "twelve years later." Again, by characterizing the poet's wife chiefly by her rhetoric, Lowell is able to magnify the threat she poses: her deceptively old-fashioned accent belies the mercilessness of her attack, an attack that not even *Miltown* can "tame."

So far I have regarded "Man and Wife" as an isolated text, and of course the poem must first of all exist in its own right. But it becomes immeasurably richer when read against the background of the adjacent poems in *Life Studies* as well as the prose autobiographical sketch "91 Revere Street," which stands at the center of the volume. Names of persons and places, settings, objects, and key incidents in one poem are woven into the total fabric, which becomes something like a novel, but a novel conceived in spatial rather than in temporal terms. In weaving together the "vast number of remembered things" (*LS*, 13), Lowell creates what Yeats called "the tradition of myself."

The prose memoir "91 Revere Street" provides the background for the painful situation described in "Man and Wife." It creates a poignant and ironic image of the tension between the poet's naval officer-father and his refined Beacon Hill mother—a tension that inevitably turns their only child into a hypersensitive, neurotic little boy. The poet places his childhood self in the center of a triangle at whose apex is the romantic figure of his ancestor, Major Mordecai Myers—dark, Mediterranean, part Jewish, "moorish-looking" —and whose base has two points, his father and mother, figures equally lifeless and futile, but strangely unlike each other and constantly at war. The theme of "91 Revere Street" and, by extension, of the whole volume, is the poet's struggle to reach the apex and move away from the Lowell-Winslow base. But he does not succeed. In "Man and Wife," the poet survives only by taking tranquillizers, and the poetic sequence culminates in the terrifying "Skunk Hour," Lowell's self-proclaimed dark night of the soul.[30]

The prose autobiography has a narrative framework, but, as in the case of the poems, its theme is conveyed not by a causally related sequence of events, but by the juxtaposition of realistic images describing the Revere Street house, the Brimmer School, the Boston Public Gardens, typical conversations, or visits from relatives. The subject matter seems Jamesian, but Lowell's style is quite unlike James's; it is, as the very title "91 Revere Street" suggests, concrete, documentary, factual, realistic.

The reference to "Mother's bed" in "Man and Wife," for example, is metonymically related to the sequence of images in the following passage, which defines Mrs. Lowell's taste in interior decorating:

Mother's comfort was chic, romantic, impulsive. If her silver service shone, it shone with hectic perfection to rebuke the functional domesticity of naval wives. She had determined to make her *ambiance* beautiful and luxurious, but wanted neither her beauty nor her luxury unaccompanied. . . . Beauty alone meant the maudlin ignominy of having one's investments managed by interfering relatives. Luxury alone, on the other hand, meant for Mother the "paste and fool's-gold polish" that one met with in

the foyer of the new Statler Hotel. She loathed the "undernourishment" of Professor Burckhard's Bauhaus modernism, yet in
moments of pique she denounced our pompous Myers mahoganies as "suitable for politicians at the Bellevue Hotel." She kept a
middle-of-the-road position, and much admired Italian pottery
with its fresh peasant colors and puritanical clean-cut lines. She
was fond of saying, "The French *do* have taste," but spoke with a
double-edged irony which implied the French, with no moral
standards to support their finish, were really no better than naval
yahoos. Mother's beautiful house was dignified by a rich veneer
of the useful.   [*LS*, 33–34]

In this passage, Mother's neurotic fear of existence is defined
metonymically by the seemingly random inventory of her
likes and dislikes in decor. Almost every possible style represents some sort of threat. Silver services that do not shine
with "hectic perfection" suggest the careless housekeeping of
naval wives, and yet the shiny "fool's-gold polish" of the Statler Hotel foyer is a sign of *nouveau riche* ostentation. "The
French *do* have taste," but they have no morals; Boston
Brahmins on the other hand have morals but no taste: their
"pompous" mahoganies are suitable only for cheap politicians. Worst of all is the "undernourishment" of modern
functionalism, espoused by such middle-European intellec-
tuals as Professor Burckhard. Having rejected the cult of
beauty that leads to genteel poverty, the luxury of the new
rich, the Bauhaus style of central Europe, the antiques of
New England, and the exquisite taste of the frivolous
French, Mother is left with nothing but her predilection for
Italian pottery. The images establish the absurdity of Mother's "ambiance": she herself emerges as the brittle little Italian urn, whose "peasant colors" have rapidly faded so that
only its "puritanical, clean-cut lines" remain.

The motif reappears in the poem "During Fever":

Mother, your master-bedroom
looked away from the ocean.
You had a window-seat,
an electric blanket,

a silver hot water bottle
monogrammed like a hip-flask,
Italian china fruity
with bunches and berries
and proper *putti.*
Gold, yellow and green,
the nuptial bed
was as big as a bathroom.   [79–80]

Mother turns her back on the ceaseless life of the ocean; she prefers the artificial "silver hot water bottle," pointlessly "monogrammed like a hip-flask," and takes refuge in her "electric blanket" and her Italian pottery, decorated with artificial fruit and "proper"—note the double meaning—*putti.* The "nuptial bed," which is, of course, the bed on which the poet and his wife recline in "Man and Wife," is "as big as a bathroom"—in other words, clean, antiseptic, and never occupied by two people at the same time.

Lowell's technique in "91 Revere Street" is to resolve the image of his mother into a series of surrounding objects or typical turns of speech. She is, for example, fond of accusing her weak husband of "backsliding" and "living in the fool's paradise of habitual retarding and retarded do-nothing inertia." Or again, she nags him into resigning from the Navy so that he will have the chance to earn more money at Lever Brothers, declaring solemnly, " 'A *man* must make up his *own* mind. Oh Bob, if you are going to resign, do it *now* so I can at least plan for your son's *survival* and education on a single continent' " (19–20).

Unaware that it is she who will not let her husband be a *man,* Mrs. Lowell is characterized by these fragments of conversation as a selfish, supercilious and embittered woman, whose air of refinement cannot mask her persistent fear of human experience. Her husband's ineffectuality is just as extreme as hers, but it is more practical, more genial, better intentioned. The following catalogue of the items in Commander Lowell's den should be read in conjunction with the account of his wife's taste in furnishings:

> The walls of Father's minute Revere Street den-parlor were bare and white. His bookshelves were bare and white. The den's one adornment was a ten-tube home-assembled battery radio set, whose loudspeaker had the shape and color of a Mexican sombrero. The radio's specialty was getting programs from Australia and New Zealand in the early hours of the morning.
>
> My father's favorite piece of den furniture was his oak and "rhinoceros hide" armchair. It was ostentatiously a masculine, or rather a bachelor's, chair. It had a notched, adjustable back; it was black, cracked, hacked, scratched, splintered, gouged, initialed, gunpowder-charred and tumbler-ringed. It looked like pale tobacco leaves laid on dark tobacco leaves. I doubt if Father, a considerate man, was responsible for any of the marring. The chair dated from his plebe days at the Naval Academy, and had been bought from a shady, shadowy, roaring character, midshipman "Beauty" Burford. Father loved each disfigured inch.   [17]

Unlike his wife, Father makes no pretense of loving luxury, beauty, or culture. The walls and bookshelves of his den are "bare and white." Rather, Commander Lowell's hobby is gadgetry: his creativity finds an outlet in assembling a ten-tube radio set, whose cute loudspeaker looks like a Mexican sombrero. The function of this radio is even more ridiculous than its appearance: it can broadcast programs from Australia and New Zealand (one wonders what programs would be coming over the air from New Zealand in the early thirties)—programs which can only be heard "in the early hours of the morning," presumably when Father is fast asleep.

The comic futility of Commander Lowell is now intensified as the focus shifts from his homemade radio to his favorite armchair, from the new gadget to the treasured "antique." No veteran of heroic naval combats, this officer comes closest to adventure in the purchase of an ugly "rhinoceros hide armchair" from that glamorous midshipman, "Beauty" Burford. Like the home-assembled radio, this chair is "unique" in a pointless way. Although it has been subject to all sorts of wear and tear, Father, who is a "considerate man," is not responsible for the spots and scratches; he would not dream of disfiguring a chair. Ironically, then, he loves the chair's aura of age and adventure, which has nothing whatever to do with him. The implication is that Father's fondness of tradition is purely surface; it is a tradition from which he himself is completely cut off. What he secretly likes best about the chair, no doubt, is the comfort of its "adjustable back" and its "ostentatiously" masculine air. Emasculated by his wife and reduced to sneaking out at night when he wants to return to the naval yard, Commander Lowell can assert his manhood only in his ridiculous affection for his "sacred 'rhino' chair."

The mode of "91 Revere Street" is essentially realistic in the sense that, as Robert Louis Jackson puts it, "our casual everyday appearance, behavior, conversation . . . contain, reflect, anticipate the larger shape of our destiny. By presenting his parents in terms of a metonymic series of objects, Lowell creates a devastating image of a tradition gone sour. Father's "rhino" chair and Mother's monogrammed hot water bottle stand metonymically for the materialistic debasement of the American dream, the dream of the Mayflower Lowells and Winslows. Given his ancestry and childhood environment, the Robert Lowell of *Life Studies* inevitably fails as a husband: the line "Tamed by *Miltown,* we lie on Mother's bed" becomes increasingly poignant when read in conjunction with its neighboring poems and with "91 Revere Street."

Whether or not the references in *Life Studies* tell "the truth" about Lowell seems beside the point. Because he is writing autobiography, Lowell cannot, of course, tinker with the basic facts of his life: geographical locale, dates, the names and positions of friends and relatives, the schools attended, the three months spent in a mental hospital, and so on. Despite such restrictions, however, Lowell has a great deal of leeway: for all we know, his mother never owned an electric blanket nor his father a "rhino" armchair; for all we know, Lowell never spent a sleepless night arguing with his wife Elizabeth. The accuracy of Lowell's confessional poetry is of interest to the biographer, but for the critic, the exciting thing is to discern how thoroughly Lowell mythologizes his private life. He begins with one established convention —the projection of the romantic lyrical "I"—and fuses the romantic "poetry of experience" with the metonymic mode perfected by the great realist novelists of the late nineteenth century. The style born of this fusion marks a turning point in the history of twentieth-century poetry.

Chapter Four

The "Life-Blood of a Poem": The Uses of Syntax

> In the working-out of a poem, I look for two things: a commanding, deadly effectiveness in the arrangement, and something that breathes and pauses and grunts and is rough and unpredictable to assure me that the journey is honest.
>
> Lowell, "On Stanley Kunitz's 'Father and Son' "

The metonymic mode of *Life Studies*—a mode which is, incidentally, prefigured in such poems as "Buttercups," "Rebellion," and "Mary Winslow" in *Lord Weary's Castle,* and which is still the dominant mode in Lowell's most recent poetry—calls for a special kind of poetic syntax, a syntax which is, interestingly, quite different from that of such other so-called confessional poets as Theodore Roethke and Sylvia Plath. Roethke's syntax illustrates admirably William E. Baker's thesis that "twentieth-century poets have markedly preferred . . . the use of fragments—usually noun phrases or clauses—not clearly related to any one sentence." [1] In "The Longing," for example, Roethke strings together series of noun phrases:

> On things asleep, no balm:
> A kingdom of stinks and sighs,
> Fetor of cockroaches, dead fish, petroleum,
> Worse than castoreum of mink or weasels,
> Saliva dripping from warm microphones,
> Agony of crucifixion on barstools. [2]

Similarly, Sylvia Plath's famous "Ariel" begins with a series of noun phrases:

Stasis in darkness.
Then the substanceless blue
Pour of tor and distances.[3]

By contrast, Lowell has, at least prior to the composition of the *Notebook* sonnets, written his poems in complete sentences, containing subject, finite verb, frequently a direct object, and almost always some phrasal or clausal modifiers. The norm, as the poet himself has insisted,[4] is that of good prose, and indeed the syntactic patterns that characterize the *Life Studies* poems are alo found in "91 Revere Street" or, for that matter, in Lowell's critical essays, which are so condensed and stylized that it is perhaps best to think of them as prose poems. In either case, the choice of syntactic structure is governed by Lowell's obsessive concern with the precise relationship of self and world, of the individual human action and the milieu in which it occurs. To qualify, to modify, to suspend the narrative movement so as to define and to discriminate—this is Lowell's syntactic impulse.

Let us begin by looking at the syntax of one of Lowell's best known poems, "Memories of West Street and Lepke":

Only teaching on Tuesdays, book-worming
in pajamas fresh from the washer each morning,
I hog a whole house on Boston's
"hardly passionate Marlborough Street,"
where even the man
scavenging filth in the back alley trash cans,
has two children, a beach wagon, a helpmate,
and is a "young Republican."
I have a nine months' daughter,
young enough to be my granddaughter.
Like the sun she rises in her flame-flamingo infants' wear.

These are the tranquillized *Fifties,*
and I am forty. Ought I to regret my seedtime?
I was a fire-breathing Catholic C. O.,
and made my manic statement,

telling off the state and president, and then
sat waiting in the bull pen
beside a Negro boy with curlicues
of marijuana in his hair.

Given a year,
I walked on the roof of the West Street Jail, a short
enclosure like my school soccer court,
and saw the Hudson River once a day
through sooty clothesline entanglements
and bleaching khaki tenements.
Strolling, I yammered metaphysics with Abramowitz,
a jaundice-yellow ("it's really tan")
and fly-weight pacifist,
so vegetarian,
he wore rope shoes and preferred fallen fruit.
He tried to convert Bioff and Brown,
the Hollywood pimps, to his diet.
Hairy, muscular, suburban,
wearing chocolate, double-breasted suits,
they blew their tops and beat him black and blue.

I was so out of things, I'd never heard
of the Jehovah's Witnesses.
"Are you a C. O.?" I asked a fellow jailbird.
"No," he answered, "I'm a J. W."
He taught me the "hospital tuck,"
and pointed out the T shirted back
of *Murder Incorporated's* Czar Lepke,
there piling towels on a rack,
or dawdling off to his little segregated cell full
of things forbidden the common man:
a portable radio, a dresser, two toy American
flags tied together with a ribbon of Easter palm.
Flabby, bald, lobotomized,
he drifted in a sheepish calm,
where no agonizing reappraisal
jarred his concentration on the electric chair—
hanging like an oasis in his air
of lost connections. . . .   [*LS*,85–86; spaced dots, Lowell's]

The diction of "Memories of West Street and Lepke" is concrete, particular, informal, and colloquial. The clothing of the poet's baby daughter, for example, is specified as "flame-flamingo infants' wear"; the view from the jail roof reveals, not simply *slums* but "sooty clothesline entanglements / and bleaching khaki tenements." Persons, places, and dates are designated with documentary precision: the poet is *forty,* he only teaches on *Tuesdays,* he lives on "Boston's / 'hardly passionate Marlborough Street,'" in his youth, he was a "Catholic C. O." and served a one-year sentence at the West Street Jail in Manhattan, where he came into contact with a Jehovah's Witness, a pacifist named Abramowitz, the "Hollywood pimps" Bioff and Brown, and finally the famous gangster Louis Lepke. The incorporation of contemporary slang or colloquialism is reflected in such phrases as "I hog a whole house," "telling off the state," "the bull pen," "I yammered metaphysics," "They blew their tops," and "I was so out of things." He refers to tranquillizers (1. 13)—the new miracle drug of the fifties—and ironically alludes to John Foster Dulles' famous phrase, "an agonizing reappraisal" (1. 50).

In contrast to the poem's almost aggressively modern vocabulary, its syntax seems fairly conventional. "Memories of West Street" contains fifteen complete sentences, ranging in length from a fraction of a line ("Ought I to regret my seedtime?"—1. 13) to eight lines (see 11. 1–8, 40–47). Although lineation is obviously essential to the poem's sound structure,[5] with respect to its syntax "Memories of West Street" could be turned into prose with almost no alterations or additions. In the first sentence (11. 1–8), for example, the only change one would make in transposing verse to conventional prose would be to add the word "and" after "Tuesdays" in line 1.

Yet despite its fidelity to a prose norm, Lowell's syntax is by no means that of ordinary speech. One notices immediately the unusual relationship of verbs to adjectivals. Critics have made much of Lowell's "harsh slamming language" with its violent, explosive verbs,[6] but, except in his most baroque poems like "The Quaker Graveyard in Nantucket" or "The Mills of the Kavanaughs," the force residing in the verbs is tempered by their context. In "Memories of West Street," there are twenty-nine verbs, seventeen of which are transitive, as compared to five intransitive and seven copulative verbs. Because the bulk of the poem (ll. 14–53) records an incident in the poet's past, nineteen of the twenty-nine verbs are in the past tense. Yet the narrative momentum of these past-tense verbs is qualified by their position, embedded as they are in a series of modifiers. In the last five lines of the poem, for example, there are two finite verbs: "drifted" and "jarred." But "he drifted" is placed directly after a series of adjectives and is followed by an adverbial phrase ("in a sheepish calm") which is in turn modified by an adjectival clause that contains the second finite verb ("jarred") and ends with the nonrestrictive participial modifier: "hanging like an oasis in his air / of lost connections." Thus the transitive force of "jarred his concentration of the electric chair" is offset. Even the stress pattern subordinates verbs to other items:

Flabby, bald, lobotomized,
he drifted in a sheepish calm.

The three unstressed syllables following "drift-" force the reader to bear down heavily on the last two words of the line: it is the "sheepish calm" and not the drifting that is emphasized.

The poem's syntactic momentum does not, then, reside in its subject-verb-object structures; it is by no means the "direct action" mode advocated by Fenollosa and Pound. There are sixty-seven adjectives, seventy-eight nouns and twenty-nine verbs in the poem. According to Josephine Miles,[7] such a ratio of adjectives to nouns, roughly five to six, and of substantives (i.e., nouns and adjectives) to predicates (i.e., verbs), roughly four to one, characterizes Lowell's style as highly *phrasal* or cumulative rather than *clausal* or discursive, although, as Miles herself demonstrates statistically, Lowell's early poetry contains a rather different proportion of the parts of speech.[8]

The heavy use of adjectivals, modifying a dynamic and concrete subject-verb unit, is, I believe, the distinctive syntactic feature of "Memories of West Street," and, for that matter, of Lowell's poetry in general. In considering the status and function of Lowell's adjectivals, we may pass over the occurrence of such single-word adjectives as *"whole* house," *"manic* statement," and *"sheepish* calm," and concentrate on Lowell's more characteristic noun modifiers. In the first place, the poet frequently uses possessive nouns where ordinary speech would demand a phrase or clause: "a *nine months'* daughter" rather than a "daughter who is nine months old," *"Murder Incorporated's* Czar Lepke" rather than "Czar Lepke, the head of *Murder Incorporated."* Second, Lowell regularly uses the noun adjunct as in *"back alley* trash cans," *"beach* wagons," *"West Street* Jail," *"school* soccer court," *"clothesline* entanglements," *"Jaundice*-yellow," *"fly-weight* pacifist," *"Hollywood* pimps," *"fellow* jailbird," *"hospital* tuck," *"toy* flags," *"Easter* palm." When it is grammatically incorrect to use a particular noun as adjunct, he turns the modifying noun into a past participle as in *"T-shirted* back." The phrase "flame-flamingo infants' wear" with its coined compound noun adjunct, followed by a possessive noun combines both methods and illustrates the poet's drive to transform other parts of speech into adjectivals.

Even more pervasive than the use of the noun adjunct is that of the present or past participle—and participial phrase

—as adjectival modifier. When such modifiers are used restrictively, Lowell observes normal word order: *"tranquillized* Fifties," *"fire-breathing* Catholic C. O.," *"bleaching* khaki tenements," *"double-breasted* suits," *"fallen* fruit," *"segregated* cell," *"lost* connections," "the man / *Scavenging filth* in the back alley trash cans," "flags *tied together,"* "things *forbidden to* the common man."

Most of the participial phrases or other adjectival modifiers are, however, used nonrestrictively. When the subject of a given sentence is a pronoun, these nonrestrictive or appositive modifiers usually precede the subject-verb unit:

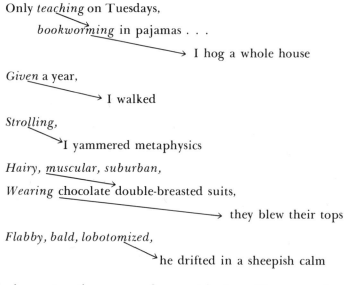

Only *teaching* on Tuesdays,

  bookworming in pajamas . . .

      → I hog a whole house

Given a year,

    → I walked

Strolling,

    ↘I yammered metaphysics

Hairy, muscular, suburban,

Wearing chocolate double-breasted suits,

       → they blew their tops

Flabby, bald, lobotomized,

     ↘he drifted in a sheepish calm

Such constructions are so frequent in Lowell's poetry that they become a kind of signature:

Fumbling for the tail-feathers of a cock,

Blue-blooded, gluttonous

    ↘it [our falcon] swallowed blood

        [*MK*, 9]

Born ten years and yet an aeon

too early for the twenties,

                → Mother, you smile   [*LS,* 80]

Tamed by Miltown

            → we lie on Mother's bed   [*LS,* 87]

Shoes off and necktie,

hunting the desired / butterfly . . .

                       → I let nostalgia drown me

                          [*FUD,* 52]

Equally frequent in "Memories of West Street" are non-restrictive adjectivals that follow the noun modified:

I have a nine-months' daughter,

            young enough to be my granddaughter

a fly-weight pacifist,

        so *vegetarian,* he wore rope shoes

Murder Incorporated's Czar Lepke,

              There *piling* towels on a rack,

            or *dawdling* off

segregated cell

        full of things forbidden to the common man

electric chair—

       hanging like an oasis in his air of lost connections

The qualification inherent in all these adjectivals is further heightened by the use of adverbs or prepositional phrases that modify the adjectivals: "*Only* teaching on Tuesdays"; "fresh from the washer *each morning,*" "young *enough* to be my granddaughter." Noun phrases in apposition also underscore the emphasis on qualification and definition:

[1]   the roof of the West Street Jail,
[2]   a short enclosure like my school soccer court

[1]   Abramowitz,
[2]   a jaundice-yellow . . . and fly-weight pacifist

Such a high degree of apposition and modification preceding and following subject and finite verb creates a peculiarly
tight, dense structure in which meanings are intensified.
Lowell avoids the excessive use of relative pronouns, auxil-
iary verbs, conjunctions, and prepositions. When the nonrestrictive modifiers precede the subject pronoun, moreover,
the meaning of the sentence is temporarily suspended so that
the reader is kept in suspense. The identity of the person
who is "Only teaching on Tuesdays" and "book-worming /
in pajamas fresh from the washer each morning," for example, is not revealed until line 3.

But the phrasal style of "Memories of West Street" has another more important function: it resolves the image of the
dramatis personae, including the "I" of the poet himself,
into a series of attributes, qualities, actions, and objects. The
syntax of the poem is thus the perfect vehicle for the realist-
confessional mode studied in the preceding chapter. In the
third stanza, for example, the "I" who is ambiguously "given
a year," rapidly becomes part of his surroundings: the roof of
the West Street Jail, whose size, shape, and outlook is described in the next five lines. Similarly, in the next sentence,
the "I" appears "Strolling" on the roof, only to fade behind
the image of his companion Abramowitz, the "jaundice-yellow" pacifist, who is, in turn, rapidly supplanted by Bioff
and Brown, the Hollywood gangsters, The seemingly gratuitous adjectival phrases characterizing these two underworld
types—"Hairy, muscular, suburban, / wearing chocolate double-breasted suits"—objectify the poet's own anxiety and
neurotic fracture. Similarly, the catalogue of items in

Lepke's cell: a "portable radio," a "dresser," "two toy American / flags tied together with a ribbon of Easter palm" metonymically stand for the debasement of the Catholic version of the American dream with its uneasy amalgam of Palm Sunday and the Fourth of July.

The syntactic structures of "Memories of West Street" thus imply that only by viewing the self in terms of its surroundings, companions, and habitual actions can the poet come to grips with the world he inhabits: the piling up of participial phrases and adjective strings guarantees the authenticity of the poet's vision. Indeed, the one passage in the poem that seems relatively flat—the sequence in lines 14–19 with its histrionic reference to the Negro boy with curlicues / of marijuana in his hair"—has a looser, paratactic syntax that is closer to everyday speech than is the rest of the poem: "I was . . . and made . . . and then sat waiting . . . ," followed by four prepositional phrases. Compared to the passage immediately following ("Given a year . . ."), this account of "waiting sentence in the bull pen" seems rather diffuse.

The syntactic patterns I have isolated in discussing "Memories of West Street" are by no means peculiar to the *Life Studies* poems, or, for that matter, to Lowell's verse. A prose passage—for example, the last paragraph of Lowell's memorial essay on Randall Jarrell, written in 1965, exhibits many of the same features:

It all comes back to me now—the just under thirty years of our friendship, mostly meetings in transit, mostly in Greensboro, North Carolina, the South he loved and stayed with, though no agrarian, but a radical liberal. Poor modern-minded exile from the forests of Grimm, I see him unbearded; slightly South American-looking, then later bearded, with a beard we at first wished to reach out our hands to and pluck off, but which later became him, like Walter Bagehot's, or some Symbolists in France's *fin de siècle* Third Republic. Then unbearded again. I see the bright, petty, pretty sacred objects he accumulated for his joy and solace: Vermeer's red-hatted girl, the Piero and Donatello reproductions, the photographs of his bruised, merciful heroes: Chekhov, Rilke, Marcel Proust. I see the white sporting Mercedes-Benz, the ever better cut and more deliberately jaunty clothes, the television with its long afternoons of professional football, those matches he thought miraculously more graceful than college football . . . Randall had an uncanny clairvoyance for helping friends in subtle precarious moments—almost always as only he could help, with something written: critical sentences in a letter, or an unanticipated published book review. Twice or thrice, I think, he must have thrown me a lifeline. In his own life, he had much public acclaim and more private. The public, at least, fell cruelly short of what he deserved. Now that he is gone. I see clearly that the spark from heaven really struck and irradiated the lines and being of my dear old friend—his noble, difficult, and beautiful soul.[9]   [spaced dots, Lowell's]

Despite its casual, informal speech ("slightly South-American looking," "modern minded," "reach out our hands to"), this passage is highly structured, perhaps even a shade mannered. Interestingly, there is at least as much ellipsis and inversion as in Lowell's poetry. In the last clause of the first sentence, for example, normal prose order would require one to say, "though *he was* no agrarian," and the third sentence, "Then unbearded again," is a fragment. At the beginning of the second sentence, Lowell introduces an elaborate inversion, a long noun phrase in apposition to the object pronoun "Him." The subject-verb-object unit "I see him" is, moreover, all but buried in a string of nonrestrictive modifiers. Preceded by the nominal "Poor modern-minded exile," it is followed by a series of adjectivals which are in turn modified by two subordinate clauses, each with its own internal modification. The resulting long (54 words) complex sentence falls into syntactic groupings whose rhythm recalls that of Lowell's free verse poems:

Poor modern-minded exile
from the forests of Grimm,
I see him
unbearded;
slightly South American-looking,
then later bearded,
with a beard
we at first wished to reach out our hands to
and pluck off,
but which later became him,
like Walter Bagehot's
or some Symbolist's
in France's fin de siecle Third Republic.

Except for the eighth line, with its surplus of function words and rather awkward final preposition, this realigned sentence may be placed side by side with Lowell's elegies on Santayana and Ford. One might note, for example, that the last line is perfect iambic pentameter except for an additional final syllable. Eight of the thirteen lines have two primary stresses. There are instances of rhyme ("Gr*imm*" / "h*im*"), alliteration ("*modern-m*inded"), assonance ("from the forests"), and consonance ("Bageho*t's* / "Symbolis*t's*"). It is, as I shall suggest later, perhaps a better "poem" than certain sonnets on Jarrell in *Notebook*.

But to return to the syntax. The phrasal qualification found in the sentence under discussion is prominent throughout the paragraph and is indeed its dominant feature. It contains thirty-eight adjectives, fifty-two nouns, and twenty-one verbs. The adjective-noun ratio, four to five, is close to that of "Memories of West Street," while the substantive-predicate ratio, four and a half to one, characterizes the prose passage as even more phrasal than the poem. The more dynamic transitive verbs are found in subordinate clauses so that their force is once again undercut: for example, "in Greensboro, North Carolina, the South he *loved*," or "I see clearly that the spark from heaven really *struck* and *irradiated* the lines and being." Action is thus subordinated to the observer's perception of it. "I see" the first-person narrator says four times, and indeed the poet's *seeing* or understanding of his friend is central to the meaning of the paragraph.

The syntactic thrust of the whole passage is, as in the case of "Memories of West Street," to resolve the general image of Jarrell into a series of concrete modifiers, defining the objects or typical actions that strike the observing "I" as central to his friend's identity. The procedure thus again involves the use of the noun adjunct (*"fin de siècle* Third Republic," "Piero and Donatello reproductions," "college football") and the possessive noun ("Walter Bagehot's," "Symbolist's," "Vermeer's"), and again the adjective series recurs.

> the bright, petty, pretty sacred objects
>
> the white sporting Mercedes Benz
>
> the ever better cut and more deliberately jaunty clothes
>
> the subtle precarious moments
>
> an unanticipated published book review
>
> his noble, difficult, and beautiful soul

Here we may observe an interesting stylistic feature. In at least three of the above examples, Lowell uses what may be termed the "false series," [10] that is, a list of items seriatim with one inharmonious term. We have already come across this device in the phrase "Hairy, muscular, suburban" in "Memories of West Street and Lepke," where the first two adjectives in no way prepare us for the third. Thus the "bright," "pretty," and "sacred" objects are also *petty;* Jarrell's "noble" and "beautiful" soul is also *difficult,* and the "ever better cut" clothes are also *deliberately jaunty,* suggesting that Jarrell is something of a poseur.

Not only adjectives but also larger phrasal units are linked together in such "false series." The first sentence illustrates Lowell's use of ambiguous syntax. It begins casually with an expletive ("It all comes back to me now") that momentarily suspends the meaning of the sentence. The main verb is followed by the subject ("the just under thirty years of our friendship"), which is in turn followed by three more noun phrases and finally by an abridged subordinate clause containing two antithetical nouns. The second phrase, "mostly meetings in transit," is grammatically in apposition to the first, but "meetings" are not parallel to "years," and we must supply a phrase like "although ours were" before the word "mostly" in order to make sense of the passage. The third noun phrase, "mostly in Greensboro, North Carolina," is connected to the second by the repetition of "mostly," but it is not an appositive, for it functions as an adverbial modifier of "in transit." Similarly, the fourth phrase is in apposition, not to the first three, but only to the words "Greensboro, North Carolina." The final adverbial clause of concession modifies "loved and stayed with." Thus each item in what seems to be a grammatically parallel series actually modifies and qualifies the preceding one:

It all comes back to me now:

[1]   the just under thirty years of our friendship,

       [although ours were]

[2]   mostly meetings in transit,
          ↑
    [3]   mostly in Greensboro, North Carolina,
              ↑
        [4]   the South he loved and stayed with,
                  ↑
            [5]   though no agrarian

                but a radical liberal.

The same strategy occurs in the fifth sentence, where "I see" is followed by a series of noun phrases, presumably constituting a compound direct object. Again there is one false member:

I see:

[1]   the white sporting Mercedes Benz,

[2]   the ever better cut and more deliberately jaunty clothes,

[3]   the television with its long afternoons of professional football

[4]   those matches he thought miraculously more graceful than college football.

"Those matches" is in apposition to "professional football," not, as the syntax would suggest, to "the television."

Such ambiguous use of apposition is not coincidental. The focus of the paragraph is on the irreconcilable elements in Jarrell's nature, the peculiar contradictions alluded to in the final phrase, "his noble, difficult, and beautiful soul." Throughout the passage, therefore, the modifiers cancel each other: Jarrell is a lover of the South who is also a radical liberal, an exile from "the forests of Grimm" who is "modern-minded," a man who cannot decide whether or not to grow a beard, whose friends cannot decide whether or not to pluck it off, a poet who loves the pure art of Vermeer and Chekhov but has a passion for fancy sports cars and televised football.

If the passage contained only a static description of Jarrell's inconsistencies, the reader's interest would soon flag,

but in fact it builds toward a definite climax. The movement
is from a general assessment of Jarrell's character to the particular value it had for Robert Lowell, the turn coming in
the sentence, "Randall had an uncanny clairvoyance for
helping friends in subtle, precarious moments." The friend
referred to is, of course, Lowell himself, and the climax
comes in the next sentence, "Twice or thrice, I think, he
must have thrown me a lifeline." This is, with respect to syllable count, the shortest sentence (13 syllables) in the paragraph. It also stands out in its spareness and simplicity: except for the brief adverbial phrase "Twice or thrice" and the
parenthetical "I think," the sentence is free of all modifiers
and uses a construction of inferred certainty:

   he   must have thrown   me   a lifeline

The judicious placing of this straightforward assertion shortly
before the conclusion, with its return to the complexity of
the beginning, seems to me uniquely Lowellian. The direct
insight that can be phrased in a simple declarative sentence
does occur, but only briefly before renewed tension, embodied in adjective strings and participial phrases, reappears.

The syntactic features discussed so far are not unique to
Lowell's later poetry; they are all contained, at least in em-
bryo, in *Lord Weary's Castle*. The two main differences—
differences which show up in a statistical study like that of
Josephine Miles [11]—are that the early poetry has a much
higher percentage of active finite verbs expressive of violent
action or motion, many in the imperative mood, than does
the later work, and that adjective clauses introduced by the
relative adverbs *where* and *when* are regularly used in cases
where Lowell would later substitute some other syntactic
form.

The dynamism of the verbs in *Lord Weary's Castle* has
often been noted and needs little further comment here.

The "drowned sailor" of "The Quaker Graveyard" "*grappled* at the net," "the winds' wings *beat upon* the stones," "The death-lance *churns* into the sanctuary, *tears* / the gun-blue swingle." Again, the "search guns" of "The Exile's Return" "*split up* timber / And *nick* the slate roofs of the Holstenwall." In "Colloquy in Black Rock," the "jack-hammer *jabs* into the ocean," and the speaker tells his heart, "you *race* and *stagger* and *demand* / More blood-gangs for your nigger-brass percussions."

Even in these early poems, however, one can discern a certain unease with such subject-verb-object constructions. In "Colloquy in Black Rock," for example, the use of transitive verbs in the first three lines quoted above gives way in lines 3–6 to the following passive locution:

> Till I, the stunned machine of your devotion,
> Clanging upon this cymbal of a hand,
> Am rattled screw and footloose.

The subject pronoun is modified, first by an appositive noun phrase (the noun is characteristically modified by a past participle) and then by a participial adjectival phrase. The main verb of the clause is a copula ("Am"), followed by the predicate adjective "rattled," with its adverbial modifiers "screw" and "footloose." The self is thus seen as acted upon rather than acting. Or, to take another example, in the opening lines of "Mr. Edwards and the Spider," the emphasis, as in the case of the Jarrell essay, is on perception, and the action resides in the participles rather than in the finite verbs:

> I saw the spiders *marching* through the air,
> *Swimming* from tree to tree that mildewed day
>   In latter August where the hay
>   Came *creaking* to the barn.   [*LWC*, 58]

Not action, but the impact of that action on the perceiving sensibility—this is the main thrust. Accordingly, the feverish imperatives ("My heart, *beat* faster, faster", "Mother, run to the chalice, and *bring back* / Blood on your finger tips," "Lord, from the lust and dust thy will destroys / *Raise* an unblemished Adam") soon disappear from Lowell's poetry. It is interesting that "The Death of the Sheriff," written later than most of the poems collected in *Lord Weary's Castle*,[12] contains almost no traces of the early hortatory, exclamatory manner.

Adjective clauses, introduced by *where* and *when,* that follow rather than precede the main clause are a hallmark of the early style. In "The Exile's Return," the first poem of *Lord Weary's Castle,* three such clauses are used in the space of twenty-four lines:

> There mounts in squalls a sort of rusty mire,
> Not ice, not snow, to leaguer the Hôtel
> De Ville, *where braced pig-iron dragons grip*
> *The blizzard in their rigor mortis.*
>
> The search-guns click and spit and split up timber
> And nick the slate roofs on the Holstenwall
> *Where torn-up tilestones crown the victor.*
>
> Past your gray, sorry and ancestral house
> *Where the dynamited walnut tree*
> *Shadows a squat, old wind-torn gate.*

"Dunbarton" has two such clauses in the first ten-line stanza:

> The stones are yellow and the grass is gray
> Past Concord by the rotten lake and hill
> *Where crutch and trumpet meet the limousine*
> And half-forgotten Starks and Winslows fill
> The granite plot and the dwarf pines are green
> From watching for the day
> *When the great year of the little yeomen come.*

Lowell continues to use these clauses in *Mills of the Kavanaughs* and *Life Studies:* "Memories of West Street," for that matter, has two:

> Marlborough Street,
> *where even the man*
> *scavenging filth in the back alley trash cans,*
> *has two children. . . .*

> he drifted in a sheepish calm,
> *where no agonizing reappraisal*
> *jarred his concentration on the electric chair.*

Such spatial and temporal qualification is, of course, essential to Lowell's metonymic mode, but for the sake of conciseness and intensity, he tends in the later poetry to replace the *where* and *when* clauses. Sometimes he substitutes for them a nominative absolute:

> Pity the planet, *all joy gone*
> from this sweet volcanic cone.   [*NO*, 24]

Sometimes a participial phrase:

> Eve and Adam, *adventuring from the ache*
> *of the first sleep,* met forms less primitive.   [*Nbk*, 29]

Occasionally a shorter independent clause:

> At last the trees are green on Marlborough Street,
> [where] *blossoms on our magnolia ignite*
> the morning.   [*LS*, 87]

Lowell's early clausal style thus gradually gives way to a predilection for modification rather than subordination, but the difference is less essential than statistics might suggest because the subordinate clauses found in the early poetry are almost always adverbial clauses of time and place, rarely clauses of concession, cause, purpose, or result. Like the phrasal modifiers that later replace them, they thus function as qualifiers, not as structures of ratiocination or argument.

The more we look at the early poetry, in fact, the more clearly we can see the beginnings of the later syntactic structure with its noun adjuncts, adjective series, long adjectival phrases preceding the noun or pronoun modified, appositive noun phrases, or nominative absolutes. Of noun adjuncts, we may cite "the peg-leg and reproachful chancellor," "parish sea," and "family-chestnut" (*LWC*, 3,7,15); "the mid-Sunday Irish," "bronze-age shards," and "bone foot" (19, 24, 54); "furnace face" and "serpent time" (69). The following phrases are good examples of adjective strings preceding the noun modified:

> Past your *gray, sorry* and *ancestral* house   [3]

> Its *escalating* and *black-windowed* blocks   [45]

> The *pale, sand-colored, treeless* chains   [57]

Or the adjective string, followed by an appositive noun phrase, may follow the noun modified:

>   our Copley ancestress,
> [*1*]   Grandiloquent, square-jowled and worldly-wise,
> [*2*]   A Cleopatra in her housewife's dress.   [25]

Or a long adjectival modifier is used to suspend meaning:

> *Beached on these dry flats of fishy real estate,*
> O Mother, I implore   [22]

> *Blacker than these black stones* the subway bends
> About the dirty elm roots.   [54]

Or an adjectival modifier is inserted between subject and predicate, as in the following example where a participial phrase is followed by a nominative absolute:

>   Hooker's heels
> [*1*]   Kicking at nothing in the shifting snow,
> [*2*]   A cannon and a cairn of cannon balls
>   Rusting before the blackened Statehouse, know
>   How the long horn of plenty broke like glass.   [17]

By the time Lowell published *Mills of the Kavanaughs* in 1951, he was using complex patterns of modification, as in the following passage from "Mother Marie Therese":

> The dead, the sea's dead, has her sorrows, [*1*] hours
> on end to lie tossing to the east, [*2*] cold,
> [*3*] without bed-fellows, [*4*] washed and bored and old,
> [*5*] Bilged by her thoughts, and [*6*] worked on by the
>   worms,
> *Until* her fossil convent come to terms
> With the Atlantic.   [*MK, 37*]

Here three lines intervene between main clause and the adverbial *"until"* clause that completes its meaning; adjectives and past participial phrases are strung together to produce a tight and dense structure.

The highly individual syntax of Lowell's poetry can be studied especially well in "After the Surprising Conversions" (LWC, 60–61), a poem so closely modeled on its source, Jonathan Edwards' "Narrative of the Surprising Conversions" (1737), [13] that the discrepancies between the two texts are especially revealing. Here, to begin with, is Edwards' first sentence, followed by Lowell's rendition of it.

Edwards:
In the latter part of May, it began to be very sensible that the Spirit of God was gradually withdrawing from us.

Lowell:
> September twenty-second, Sir: today
> I answer. In the latter part of May,
> Hard on our Lord's Ascension, it began
> To be more sensible.

Not only does Lowell revise in the direction of concreteness (he begins on an abrupt personal note and specifies the date [14]), but, more important, he immediately gets rid of Edwards' subordinate "that" clause and adds a specifying adjectival phrase modifying "the latter part of May." The result is that Lowell's lines are at once more precise and more mysterious than is Edwards' sentence: we know exactly when "it began to be more sensible," but we don't yet know what "it" refers to and so are in suspense.

The transformation of Edwards' third sentence is even more striking.

Edwards:
He was a Gentleman of more than common Understanding, of strict Morals, religious in his Behaviour, and an useful honourable Person in the Town; but was of a Family that are exceeding prone to the Disease of Melancholy, and his Mother was killed with it.

Lowell:
>   A gentleman
>   Of more than common understanding, strict
>   In morals, pious in behavior, kicked
>   Against our goad. A man of some renown,
>   An useful, honored person in the town,
>   He came of melancholy parents; prone
>   To secret spells, for years they kept alone—
>   His uncle, I believe, was killed of it:
>   Good people, but of too much or little wit.

Here Lowell retains all the ideas in Edwards' complex declarative sentence (although he replaces the sinner's mother by his uncle) and much of his phrasing, but he transforms the syntax completely. First, he lops off the initial "He was" so that "A Gentleman" becomes the subject of "kicked against our goad," a dynamic and concrete predicate which is purely Lowell's invention. Then he takes Edwards' second predicate nominative, "an useful honourable Person in the town," and places it, together with a second noun phrase of his own invention, at the beginning of a new sentence where both noun phrases function as appositives, preceding the subject pronoun "He":

[1]   A man of some renown,
[2]   An useful, honored person in the town,
       He . . .

Moreover, Lowell turns the subordinate clause "that are exceeding prone to the Disease of Melancholy" into a phrasal construction in which the adjectival modifier again precedes the subject pronoun: "prone to secret spells, for years *they* kept alone." Finally, we may note that Lowell adds a parenthetical noun phrase, not found in Edwards' text, as an appositive to "melancholy parents": "Good people, but of too much or little wit."

It would be tedious to go through the whole poem making such point by point comparisons, and I will confine myself to only one more example, lines 39–43 of "After the Surprising Conversions."

Edwards:
And many that seemed to be under no Melancholy, some pious Persons, that had no special Darkness, or Doubts about the goodness of their State, nor were under special Trouble or Concern of Mind about anything Spiritual or Temporal, yet had it urged upon 'em, as if somebody had spoken to 'em, *Cut your own-Throat, now is a good Opportunity. Now; now!*

Lowell:
>   The multitude, once unconcerned with doubt,
>   Once neither callous, curious nor devout,
>   Jumped at broad noon, as though some peddler groaned
>   At it in its familiar twang: "My friend,
>   Cut your own throat. Cut your own throat. Now! Now!"

Again Lowell's revision is more concrete and idiomatic ("Jumped at broad noon," "some peddler groaned," "familiar twang"), and again the main syntactic revision is to remove the subordinate "that . . ." clauses and replace them with shorter adjectival phrases modifying the noun "multitude." The first is a passive participial construction ("once unconcerned with doubt"), the second, Lowell's familiar adjective string ("neither callous, curious, nor devout"). The repetition of "once" points up the temporal gap between "then" and "now," and indeed throughout the poem Lowell is careful to provide time signals: "September 22," "today," "in the latter part of May," "one Sabbath," "broad noon," and so on. In the last three lines of the poem, which have no counterpart in Edwards' text, Lowell repeats the date, uses a noun adjunct ("the small-mouth bass"), and concludes with a passive participial phrase in dislocated position: "The small-mouth bass breaks water, *gorged with spawn.*"

Lowell's rendition of Edwards' "Narrative of the Surprising Conversions" seems to me much more successful than the translation of Rimbaud discussed in Chapter Two because here the alterations are basically syntactic rather than semantic. Edwards' central meaning remains intact, but the heroic verse frame, the concreteness and specificity of diction, and the condensation that results from the transformation of subordinate relative or causative clauses into adjectival modifiers or appositives create a peculiarly dynamic and tightly woven structure.

But what happens when the modifiers no longer modify anything? In the *Notebooks,* Lowell's predilection for the phrasal style becomes more and more pronounced, and the subject-verb units, which were formerly embedded in a network of surrounding adjectivals, now disappear completely. Here, for example, is the first version of one of the *Randall Jarrell* sonnets:

> Grizzling up the embers of our onetime life,
> our first intoxicating disenchantments,
> dipping our hands once, twice, in the same river,
> entrained for college on the Ohio local;
> the scene shifts, middle distance, back and foreground,
> things changing position like chessmen on a wheel,
> drawn by a water buffalo, perhaps
> blue with true space before the dawn of days—
> then the night of the caged squirrel on its wheel:
> lights, eyes, peering at you from the overpass;
> black-gloved, black-coated, you plod out stubbornly,
> as if asleep, Child Randall, as if in chainstep,

> meeting the cars, and approving; with harsh
> luminosity grasping at the blank coin of the tunnel.

[Nbk, 67, 24]

One notes immediately that the ratio of parts of speech has altered in the decade since Lowell wrote *Life Studies*. In this particular sonnet, there are thirty-two nouns, twenty-four adjectives, and only two finite verbs, so that the ratio of substantives to predicates is almost thirty to one. The sestet, with its account of Jarrell's tragic suicide, is the heart of the poem. Lowell introduces this sequence with a nominal phrase: "then the night of the caged squirrel on its wheel," and then rapidly sketches in the setting, using a nominative absolute construction: "Lights, eyes, peering at you from the overpass." Now Jarrell the pedestrian appears on the scene:

> black-gloved,
> black-coated,
>
> you plod out stubbornly,
> as if asleep . . .
> as if in chainstep,
>
> meeting the cars . . .
> approving . . .
> grasping at the blank coin of the tunnel.

Here the modifiers create a most effective ambiguity. "Black-gloved, black-coated" suggests that Jarrell knows he is going to his own funeral and has dressed accordingly, but the abridged clauses, "as if asleep, as if in chainstep," imply that perhaps the poet has no real volition, that he is sleepwalking to his death. The three active participial phrases that conclude the poem do not provide the reader with a clear-cut answer; rather, they present the immediacy of the act itself: the underlying despair that draws Jarrell to the ghostly "blank coin" at the end of the dark tunnel.

But I am not sure that the octave is as carefully rendered. The first four lines contain a series of three participial phrases in parallel sequence:

Grizzling . . .
dipping . . .
entrained . . .

But syntax and meaning are insufficiently related: the two poets are remembering their "first intoxicating enchantments," and "grizzling"—bringing back to life—the embers of their past, in the *present,* whereas they were "dipping" their hands in the river and being "entrained for college" in the distant *past.* Since the poem stresses the revivifying force of memory and the distinction between a bleak present and a joyful past, one wonders why Lowell put the three participles in parallel construction. Moreover, because the second two phrases do not modify anything, the reader is left hanging. What about these young men dipping their hands "once, twice, in the same river"? What does the ritual signify? And what was the special charm or significance of the Ohio local which took them to college? [15] How do these past experiences foreshadow or relate to the "night of the caged squirrel"—the suicide act? When Lowell breaks off his syntactic construction in line 5 with the phrase "the scene shifts," he seems to be taking the easy way out. Nor is the oriental scene of lines 5–8, with its water buffalo drawing, its chessman-like figures that change position in an eternally blue prehistoric space, sufficiently coordinated with the other images. Past and present remain isolated from one another, imprisoned in their respective sentence fragments.

There are indeed beautiful fragments in *Notebook* but very few fully articulated poems. The imagery, as I suggested in Chapter One, is consistent with that of the earlier poetry, and accordingly, when one confines oneself to a study of imagery, the defects in *Notebook* are not readily apparent. But the new loose syntax is problematic.

The fourth sonnet in the "Harvard" sequence, for instance, like "Memories of West Street and Lepke," begins with a series of participial phrases:

> *Inching* along the bayfront on the icepools,
> sea and shipping *cut out* by the banks of cars
> and our relationship *advancing* or
> *declining* to private jokes, and chaff and lust. . . .
>
> [*Nbk,* 80; spaced dots, Lowell's]

But whereas in "Memories of West Street" the introductory phrases are closely related to the main clause, "I hog a whole house . . . ," the sequence of modifiers in the Harvard sonnet merely trails off with a series of dots so that it is impossible to tell what relevance the bayfront traffic jam has to the current relationship of the lovers. Rather, the poet's consciousness abruptly switches back to the past as he explains—seemingly to the reader rather than to his companion—that he must seize the moment because their former meetings were always hurried, interrupted, or disturbed:

> Our leeway came so seldom, fell so short,
> overwatched by some artist's skylight in the city,
> or some suburban frame-house basement window,
> angular, night-bluish, blear-eyed, spinsterish.

Here the adjective series—a favorite Lowellian device—has become a mere mannerism.[16] Why is the basement window envisioned as a threatening presence, "angular, night-bluish, blear-eyed, spinsterish"? Evidently because suburban frame houses are the enemy of clandestine romantic idylls! But even if we accept this cliché as somehow valid, why are these lovers better off in a car, caught in a traffic jam? When one remembers the discriminating use of the adjective series in *Life Studies* and *For the Union Dead*—Grandmother's "lavender mourning and touring veil" (*LS,* 68); the alley of poplars, "Diamond-pointed, athirst, and Norman" at Grandfather Winslow's farm (*LS,* 59); or the "dark downward and vegetating kingdom / of the fish and reptile" in the "old South Boston Aquarium" (*FUD,* 70), the difference is striking. In the earlier poetry, the adjective strings metonymically define Lowell's world; here, the poet all too often uses adjectives out of sheer habit. Thus Mary McCarthy's house has an "eight-inch, star-blue, softwood floorboard" (*Nbk,* 33); the poet crosses Central Park in his "Dickensian muffler, snow-sugared, unraveling"; he has a "candlelight lunchdate" in "An oldtime sweatshop remodelled, purple brick"; and he observes the peacemarchers reeling down the street, "bellbottom, barefoot, Christendom's wild hair" (*Nbk* 110, 86, 71). Many of these references are gratuitous: it does not really matter that the old sweatshop is "purple brick," and we take it for granted that the bellbottomed peacemarchers are barefoot and have wild hair.

The increasing reliance on apposition also produces a certain flatness. The fourth sonnet in "Long Summer" is made up of noun phrases separated by semicolons:

> The vaporish closeness of this two-month fog;
> thirty-five summers back, the brightest summer:
> the Dealer's Choice, the housebound girls, the fog;
> fog lifting. Then, as now, the after curfew
> boom of an unknown nightbird, local hemlock
> gone black as Roman cypress, the barn-garage
> below the tilted Dipper lighthouse-white,
> a single misanthropic frog complaining
> from the water hazard on the shortest hole;
> till morning! Short dreams, short shrift—one second, bright
> as burning shavings, scattered bait and ptomaine
> caught by the gulls with groans like straining rope;
> windjammer pilgrims cowled in rubber hoods,
> making for harbor in their yellow bus.   [*Nbk,* 26]

Here it seems to me that Lowell omits the very connectives we need in order to understand the poem and puts in modifiers that we don't really need. In line 11, the poet wants to show that like "Short dreams," burning shavings are "bright" for only a second before they become "scattered bait" for gulls. But there is no punctuation or connective phrase (e.g., "the next" or "and then") between "burning shavings" and "scattered bait." Again in line 13, "windjammer pilgrims" seems to be in apposition to "gulls with groans" when in fact the poet is saying something like "victims of the fog world, we are like windjammer pilgrims," or "look at the windjammer pilgrims." On the other hand, such appositives as "the Dealer's Choice" don't really enrich our image of "the brightest summer," nor does it help to know that the "local hemlock" looks as black as a Roman cypress, or that the garage, strangely floodlit by the "tilted Dipper," is a former barn. It seems as if every noun must be modified by an adjective or compounded with another noun, whether or not such complication is integral to the poem's total structure.

Notebook contains too many poems written too hastily, and because Lowell restricts himself to the fourteen-line iambic pentameter norm of the sonnet, he must do a lot of padding. Nevertheless, the signature of the great craftsman is still present. We may conclude our analysis of the poet's syntax by looking at "Nesting," which first appeared in the expanded 1970 edition of *Notebook:*

> Discovering, discovering trees are green at night,
> braking headlights-down, ransacking the roadside
> for someone strolling, fleeing to her wide goal;
> passing blanks, the white Unitarian Church,
> dark barn on my bulwark, two scowling unlit shacks,
> the town pool just drained, the white lighthouse unplugged,
> watching the beerfroth on the muddy breakers,
> dwarfed by the STATE OF MAINE, white iceberg at dry-
>   dock.
> The question, my questioners? It's not for them—
> crouched in the gelid drip of the pine in our garden,
> invisible even when found, till we toss a white raincoat
> over your sky-black, blood-trim quilted stormcoat—
> you saying *I would prefer not,* like Bartleby:
> small deer tremble and steely in wet nest!   [*Nbk,* 224]

This sonnet records a fairly ordinary experience: a father's anxious search for his daughter who has run away from home, and the relief he experiences when he finally finds her right in her own backyard. The frenzied nightride is conveyed in a series of participial phrases that make up the octave:

> *Discovering, discovering* trees are green at night
> *braking* headlights-down
> *ransacking* the roadside for someone strolling
> > > *fleeing* toward her goal
> *passing* blanks: the white Unitarian Church
> > > dark barn on my bulwark
> > > two scowling unlit shacks
> > > the town pool just drained
> > > white lighthouse unplugged
> *watching* the beerfroth on the muddy breakers,
> > > dwarfed by the STATE OF MAINE,
> > > > white iceberg at drydock.

Here the present participles convey the violent speed of the speaker's car as it passes a series of "blanks" or structures now emptied of their familiar content: the swimming pool is literally emptied, the lighthouse is emptied of its familiar light, and the ocean itself is "emptied" by the shadow of that looming iceberg, the STATE OF MAINE at drydock. The normal everyday, daytime world is thus turned upside-down in the speaker's vision.

The sestet presents the resolution of the conflict as the active participial phrases of the octave give way to passive constructions. The newly found girl and her father face the Questioners in the form of local police or rescue squad. Like Melville's Bartleby, the little girl prefers not to explain her actions and motives to those who could never understand them anyway, and her father wisely does not force her to respond: his words of dismissal, "It's not for them," constitute the only complete declarative sentence in the poem. The child is seen:

crouched in the gelid drip of the pine in our garden,
invisible even when found till we toss a white raincoat
over your sky-black, blood-trim quilted stormcoat.

The word "quilted" seems gratuitous in the context, and the
suggestion that the stormcoat's dark red trim is analogically
the blood of the hunted little animal has a vaguely porten-
tous air. But the reference to the blackness of the stormcoat
is wholly integral: like the lighthouse the child is "un-
plugged," needing the protection of the white raincoat in
order to become a familiar object. Once she is covered by
this talisman, she is once again alive and vulnerable—a
small deer, "tremble and steely in wet nest."

At his best, Lowell is a superb manipulator of the telling
adjective, the modifying phrase, the qualifying participial
construction. The placement of highly concrete and colloquial diction and specific graphic images in tightly woven
structures of modification creates a condensed, packed,
highly charged verbal style that is uniquely Lowellian. In
his best poetry, the dynamism of finite verbs is nicely balanced by the qualifying phrasal modifiers. Only when this
balance is offset, when Lowell begins to imitate himself, piling up gratuitous adjective strings and adjectival phrases
that do not relate to a central subject-verb-object kernel,
does the style go slack. The poetic cosmos remains intact,
but when the syntactic structures fail to measure its dimen-
sions, its outlines become blurred.

Chapter Five

The Voice of the Poet:
The Winslow Elegies

> The earthbound event which meant most to the Puritan
> was death. His life was harder than that of most men of
> his time; as a pioneer, he was overbearingly aware of the
> dangers to body and soul of his enterprise. . . . His most
> important poems are called forth by the ever-threatening
> imminence of death. These poems are elegies—lengthy,
> discursive and elevated—most often on the death of good
> men and powerful. . . . For the occasion of a death, the
> point just before the final proof of election or damnation,
> gave the Puritan poet his greatest opportunity. Now a man
> newly dead would really *know*. And the poet would bear
> witness to that knowledge, if only he could work out the
> way of getting it.
>
> Roy Harvey Pearce, *The Continuity of American Poetry* [1]

One of Roy Harvey Pearce's examples of the Puritan poetic meditation on dèath is a late seventeenth-century elegy
on William Bradford by Josiah Winslow.[2] In 1944, nearly
300 years later, Josiah Winslow's descendant, Robert Lowell,
wrote an elegy on his grandfather Arthur Winslow, in which
the Puritan tradition of the New England Winslows is cate-
gorically rejected by a poet who paradoxically is himself, in
the words of his friend and fellow-poet Randall Jarrell, "the
ideal follower of Barth and Calvin." [3] Surely no other modern American poet has been as obsessed with death and last
things as has Lowell: from *Land of Unlikeness* (1944) to
Notebook (1970), his most characteristic and celebrated
poems have been elegies, particularly elegies on his maternal
or Winslow relatives.[4]

The subject matter of these elegies has remained remarkably constant during Lowell's career to date. They are therefore a particularly good place to explore the greatest variable in Lowell's poetry: the manipulation of the speaking voice. To study the changes in tone in the Winslow elegies is to become aware of the tremendous effort Lowell has evidently made to overcome an instinctive tendency to quarrel with others rather than with himself, to substitute invective and declamatory scorn for poetry. At the height of his career—in the decade that produced *Life Studies* and *For the Union Dead*—Lowell managed, in Irvin Ehrenpreis' words, "to infuse the despair of his disgust with the humour of his irony." [5] The speaker of these poems is a self-searching and self-critical "I" who can laugh at his own foibles and is content to understand others rather than to judge them. But in the subsequent poetry, collected in *Near the Ocean* and *Notebook,* Lowell often reverts to his earlier stance as disdainful preacher-poet who regards the lives of his dead relatives as so many exempla of the ultimate failure of the New England Puritan vision. Thus, although the righteous indignation of the young poet who addresses his grandfather in "In Memory of Arthur Winslow" has given way, by the late sixties, to the rather weary sarcasm of "Fourth of July in Maine," [6] the poems suffer from a similar failure to integrate the voices of satire and elegy. These two elegies may, in fact, be seen as the two low points on a parabola, at whose top we may place such Winslow elegies as "My Last Afternoon with Uncle Devereux Winslow" and "Soft Wood," which are among the great poems of our time.

"In Memory of Arthur Winslow"

Critics have generally praised "In Memory of Arthur Winslow" as one of Lowell's finest early poems.[7] Jerome Mazzaro, for example, admires the poem's "successful interplay . . . of personal and traditional levels," and observes that in the final section, "theology, liturgy, mythology, history and personal observation are fused." [8] Similarly, Hugh Staples comments, "In the fine elegy to his grandfather . . . Lowell displays, in a sustained effort, his astonishing ability to move with ease from the moral geography of Boston . . . to the cosmic scene, in which symbolism from both Christian and pagan traditions are harmoniously fused." [9]

The metrical form of "In Memory of Arthur Winslow" has also been praised. As Allen Tate pointed out in his introduction to *Land of Unlikeness*, every poem in the book has a strict formal pattern either invented by Lowell or borrowed from other poets. [10] In this case, the stanza form is derived from Matthew Arnold's "The Scholar Gypsy": each iambic pentameter stanza has ten lines rhyming *abcbcadeed;* in each case, the sixth line is shortened to three stresses. This strict metrical form is, according to Staples, an excellent means of controlling the violence of the imagery (p. 19).

"Fusion" and "control" are, however, strange terms to apply to an elegy that fails to fulfill the most basic requirements of the form: it contains no lament and a very dubious consolation. [11] Although the poet announces that he has come to mourn and to memorialize his grandfather, he ends by attacking him, dwelling on his sins, and implying that, as a representative of his social class and religious sect, Arthur Winslow is one of the damned.

The poem is divided into four parts. [12] In the first, "Death from Cancer," the speaker addresses his grandfather directly. Cruelly honest, he morbidly tells the dying man that it is useless to wrestle with the "crab":

> The claws drop flesh upon your yachting blouse
> Until longshoreman Charon come and stab
> Through your adjusted bed
> And crush the crab.   [*LWC,* 19]

The reference to Charon, the terrible ferryman who rows the souls of the dead across Acheron, the river of woe, into the underworld, implies that Winslow's death is a prelude to greater suffering, an implication borne out by lines 9–10: "You ponder why the coxes' squeakings dwarf / The *resurrexit dominus* of all the bells." Because he has no true Christian faith, Arthur cannot penetrate the mystery of the *resurrexit dominus*. The first stanza, then, already suggests that Arthur's death will not lead to his salvation.

In the second stanza, after reminding his grandfather, with a slight touch of malice, that the Public Gardens of Boston have been taken over by the "mid-Sunday Irish," the poet suddenly switches to the third person and asserts that

> the ghost
> Of risen Jesus walks the waves to run
> Arthur upon a trumpeting black swan
> Beyond Charles River to the Acheron
> Where the wide waters and their voyager are one.

Mazzaro observes, "With 'trumpeting black swan' Lowell reinserts the classical idea that a swan utters a cry before death, and here, with 'trumpeting' rather than 'honking,' he further suggests that Winslow would be welcomed in heaven. . . . In conjunction with death, the swan also invites a favorable comparison of the qualities of King Arthur with those of Arthur Winslow, whose journey to afterlife resembles that of the monarch's epic swan journey to Avalon" (p. 8).

This interpretation may well reflect Lowell's intentions, but it does not explain how the swan symbolism is related to the other images in the poem or why the muddy waters of Boston Basin and the Charles River are suddenly transformed into the miraculous waves on which Christ walks. Mazzaro himself reminds us that "The faithful called over the Acheron succeed in crossing the water to heaven only while they, like Peter in the water-walking episode in the Bible, have faith in Christ" (p. 9). But, as the first stanza has implied and as the rest of the poem will make clear, Arthur

Winslow did not have faith in Christ. How then can he cross the "wide waters" of the Acheron to heaven? And how does the speaker *know* with such assurance what Arthur's fate will be?

The poem never comes to terms with these questions; the salvation theme is abruptly dropped, and in Part II, "Dunbarton," Arthur Winslow's burial is rendered with cruel and disenchanted precision. The cold "granite plot" of the "half-forgotten Starks and Winslows" at Dunbarton symbolizes the spiritual aridity of the New England Puritan tradition. The speaker is revolted by what he sees: at his grandfather's funeral, thoughts of the dead man are obscured by his agonized perception of his living relatives, arriving in limousines with their crutches, both physical and mental, in order to perform their hollow rites in this landscape with its "gray" grass, "yellow" stones, and "rotten" lake. Even the "dwarf pines" (everything looks "dwarfed" to the jaundiced eye of the speaker) are envious ("green") of their more robust ancestors as they wait pointlessly for the "landed Promise" of the Mayflower Compact, a promise that has never been fulfilled.

In the second stanza of "Dunbarton," the speaker addresses his ancestors directly: "Oh fearful witnesses, your day is done." The faith of the Pilgrim Fathers, the religious zeal that once made them "point their wooden steeples lest the Word be dumb," is dead; in modern Boston, the Protestant creed is reduced to empty posturing: "The preacher's mouthings still / Deafen my poor relations on the hill." The relations are "poor" because they have no faith; only a "cold sun" "melts" on his grandfather's casket and the graves of the unbelieving, materialistic Winslows are viewed as "sunken landmarks."

The usual reading of "Dunbarton" as the devout Catholic's critique of the shortcomings of Protestant theology [13] ignores the poem's tone. The angry and oracular voice that delivers the denunciation is strangely reminiscent of the voice of Jonathan Edwards in "Mr. Edwards and the Spider," informing his relative, Josiah Hawley, that, struggle though he may, he is predestined to eternal damnation:

> It was in vain you set up thorn and briar
>   In battle array against the fire
>   And treason crackling in your blood;
>   For the wild thorns grow tame
>   And will do nothing to oppose the flame;
>   Your lacerations tell the losing game
>   You play against a sickness past your cure.
>   How will the hands be strong? How will the heart endure?
>
> [LWC, 58]

"Mr. Edwards and the Spider" and its companion piece, "After the Surprising Conversions," succeed because Lowell uses the persona of Edwards to dramatize the peculiarly Puritan dilemma in which the sinner must confront the truth of the angry God directly, with no mediator, "no middle term, no gentle order, no Christ." [14] In using the mask of Edwards, Lowell lets the situation speak for itself; we *see* what it means for the isolated self to cower before a cruel God. But when Lowell uses the voice of the Calvinist preacher to castigate Calvinist preachers and to berate his Calvinist ancestors, the prevailing impression is one of confusion rather than fusion. Elegy traditionally contains satiric attacks on certain groups hostile to the dead man commemorated—the clergy in "Lycidas," the reviewers in "Adonais"—but in "In Memory of Arthur Winslow," the subject of the elegy, Winslow himself and the tradition he stands for, is under attack.

The same indignant moral tone prevails in Part III, "Five Years Later," Paraphrasing Mark Antony, the speaker says, "This Easter, Arthur Winslow, five years gone / I came to mourn you, not to praise the craft / That netted you a million dollars," but we look in vain for the promised lament.

Instead, this section of the elegy specifies the sin that removed Arthur from Christianity—his materialistic greed, which brought him to Colorado in search of gold. Arthur's name is linked to that of Cotton Mather as well as to those of earlier Winslows: Edward (1595–1655), the sometime governor of Plymouth, who came over on the Mayflower and built the "blockhouse" mentioned in line 12; his grandson Edward (1669–1753), a well-known sheriff and silversmith; and General John Stark (1728–1822), the Revolutionary War general who founded the township of Dunbarton.[15] All these men shared Arthur Winslow's materialism and ambition, but at least they made substantial contributions to the government and cultural life of America, whereas the poet's grandfather achieved no fame outside the family circle and is remembered by the speaker as one whose thirst for wealth was his ruling passion. The harshness of the speaker's judgment is intensified by the direct address to Grandfather Winslow, now "five years dead." Even standing beside the grave on Easter Sunday, the poet can neither forget nor forgive.

Part IV, "A Prayer for My Grandfather to Our Lady," seems to provide a conventional consolation motif. Images of salvation are now introduced. Staples points out that "the poet, in his role of mediator, puts the words from the *Miserere* (slightly altered from *me* to an inclusive *nos*) into Latin: *Lavabis nos et super nivem dealbabor,* in his effort to effect a kind of posthumous conversion" (p. 30). Again, however, the overall emphasis of this section is less on conversion than on sin and destruction, Jonathan Edwards' ruling themes. The speaker begins by telling Our Lady that "Neither my father nor his father" with their "clippers" and "slavers"—symbols of materialistic exploitation—have reached "The haven of your peace." This categorical statement comes dangerously close to asserting Grandfather Winslow's damnation. The prayer that follows is less a prayer for Arthur Winslow than for the poet himself:

Beached

On these dry flats of fishy real estate,
O Mother, I implore
Your scorched, blue thunderbreasts of love to pour
Buckets of blessings on my burning head
Until I rise like Lazarus from the dead.   [*LWC,* 22]

Marius Bewley writes of this passage, "This is a network of conflicting connotations that operates at cross-purposes. 'Thunderbreasts' . . . is meant to suggest the mythical Thunderbird of various Indian tribes which was supposed to bring rain, and so the word may imply the life-giving qualities of Our Lady's love. But Our Lady and the Thunderbird . . . belong to traditions too remote to coalesce imaginatively." As for the phrase "Buckets of blessings on my burning head," it suggests that "Our Lady is dousing a halo." [16]

This verbal confusion (what Bewley calls the "Gilbert and Sullivan" quality of the passage) reflects the larger structural irresolution of the poem. The "Prayer for My Grandfather" begins as a diatribe against him and then turns inward upon the speaker, the *lavabis nos* notwithstanding. The Puritan habit of tortuous introspection to determine whether one is to be among the elect or the damned collides with the professed Catholic prayer. In the second stanza, moreover, Lowell suggests that the stained glass windows of the Protestant Trinity Church in Boston represent the limits of Winslow's religious faith; the "painted Paradise of harps and lutes," reminiscent of the painted city of Babylon, must sink like Atlantis, the symbol of materialism, into the Devil's jaw.[17] Grandfather Winslow's weak Protestantism, a ceremony without faith, is thus doomed.

Mazzaro holds that line 15, "And knock the Devil's teeth out by the roots," is the crucial line: "this sinking will defeat the Devil for teeth are regenerative organs" (p. 18). Salvation is, in other words, reaped out of destruction. But whose salvation is in question? The "I" now comes into the fore-

ground as the anguished speaker "strikes for shore." [18] For
him, religion is not just a matter of "painted idols"; he begs
the Blessed Mother to "run to the chalice and bring back /
Blood on your fingertips for Lazarus who was poor." Lowell
here employs a double Biblical allusion, to both the Lazarus
of Luke 16 : 19–31 and the more famous Lazarus of John II.
It can be argued, as Mazzaro does (p. 98), that Lowell ironically reverses the positions of the rich and the poor man in
Luke, so that the "poor Lazarus" for whom Christ must intercede is none other than the rich Arthur Winslow. But if
the meaning of Stanza II is thus that Winslow will be saved
by Christ after all, it is hardly stated very forcefully. On the
contrary, the syntax of the passage suggests that the poet
himself rather than his grandfather is the "Lazarus who was
poor"; the movement of the elegy is, consequently, a sudden
leap from a condemnation of Arthur Winslow to a final
prayer for the speaker's salvation.

"In Memory of Arthur Winslow" is ultimately a flawed
poem because one is never sure whether it is social criticism
or elegy; tone and theme clash throughout. The larger structure does not cohere because there is no relationship between the final prayer to Our Lady and the blistering attacks
on Winslow piety in Part II and on Winslow materialism in
Part III. The ambivalent use of water imagery is an index to
this basic irresolution. To the unbeliever, Arthur Winslow,
water is an indifferent natural element: it is Boston Basin,
where the "clippers" and "slavers" of his ancestors satisfied
their greed, it is the "sun-struck shallows" where the "mid-
Sunday Irish" fish for chub, it is the "rotten lake" at Dunbarton. To the Christian speaker, water is the symbol of salvation: the waves where "the ghost of risen Jesus walks," the
"wide waters" to which the "trumpeting black swan" brings
the soul of Arthur Winslow, the "buckets of blessing on my
burning head," and the *lavabis nos* of the liturgy. But these
two contradictory symbolic meanings of water are never rec-

onciled or even related within the elegy, in which the poet alternately judges others and prays that their fate will not be his. In his perceptive review of *Land of Unlikeness,* R. P. Blackmur made a comment that nicely sums up the problem: "In dealing with men his [Lowell's] faith compels him to be fractiously vindictive, and in dealing with faith his experience of men compels him to be nearly blasphemous. . . . What is thought of as Boston in him fights with what is thought of as Catholic; and the fight produces not a tension but a gritting." [19]

"The Quaker Graveyard in Nantucket"

In his second major elegy, "The Quaker Graveyard in Nantucket," Lowell consciously tried to move from the personal to the impersonal or mythic mode that one associates with Eliot. Not only is Warren Winslow, Lowell's young cousin killed in World War II, who is the nominal subject of the elegy, hardly felt as a presence in the poem, but the narrator now recedes as well. The occasional use of direct impassioned address to the sailor, as in the lines, "All you recovered from Poseidon died / With you my cousin" (*LWC,* 10), is subordinated to an impersonal vision of the terrible effects of spiritual alienation at any moment in history. Ahab's whale hunt in *Moby Dick* is used in the elegy as the central symbol of man's attempt to abuse his dominion over nature.

Of all Lowell's poems, this is the one most frequently and fully explicated,[20] and another complete reading would be superfluous. What is important for our purpose is that, although Lowell here avoids the embarrassingly self-righteous tone of his earlier elegy and does not attack Warren Winslow personally, he still has great difficulty in articulating the total structure of the elegy. Like "In Memory of Arthur Winslow," "The Quaker Graveyard" contains no lament, and again the consolation, this time explicitly placed in Section VI, "Our Lady of Walsingham," is not integrated into the poem, which deals with the rapacity and greed of the New England Protestants of the nineteenth century, who are linked in Lowell's mind to the modern patriotic capitalists, here represented by Warren Winslow, who fought for a meaningless cause in World War II.

"The Quaker Graveyard" has frequently been compared to "Lycidas." [21] Hugh Staples lists the following parallels: the death of a young man to whom the poet has a more than casual yet less than intimate relationship, death by drowning, the unrecovered body, the movement beyond the lament to a larger consideration of contemporary and universal issues, and the "answer to the apparent futility of a young man's death, but in terms of Catholic mysticism rather than through the more or less orthodox Protestant solution of Milton." Both Lowell and Milton draw upon classical and Biblical sources for their patterns of imagery; both pay indirect homage to great figures in their native traditions— Thoreau and Melville in Lowell's case; Theocritus, Bion, and Virgil in Milton's. Both use place names to evoke the *genius loci:* for the Hebrides, Namancos, and Bayona, Lowell substitutes Nantucket, Martha's Vineyard, and Walsingham (pp. 45–46). Even the verse form of "The Quaker Graveyard" resembles that of "Lycidas": its 194 lines are "divided like the 193 lines of 'Lycidas' into a loose structure of pentameter lines, varied by an occasional trimeter. Each stanza has its own highly intricate rhyme scheme, repeated in only two cases (Stanzas II and VII), yet differing from each other only slightly. Like Milton, then, Lowell adapts the *canzone* form to his own uses" (p. 45).

Yet surely the differences between the two elegies outweigh these superficial similarities. Whether we think of "Lycidas" as a symphony, as does Marjorie Nicolson,[22] or as a rondo, as does Northrop Frye,[23] its structure is "musical" in that the motifs of lament and consolation, introduced in the opening lines of the poem with the symbolism of myrtle and laurel, "echo antiphonally" [24] throughout the elegy so that the final climactic affirmation, "Weep no more, woeful shepherds, weep no more, / For Lycidas, your sorrow, is not dead," has been prepared for all along.

There is no such contrapuntal development in "The Quaker Graveyard." Lowell's elegy begins on a note of horror: the epigraph from Genesis, "Let man have dominion over the fishes of the sea and the fowls of the air and the beasts, and the whole earth, and every creeping creature that moveth upon the earth," is an ironic commentary on the awful abuse of this privilege by the Quaker whalers and their Godless modern descendants. What follows is a powerfully concrete description of death at sea.[25] The "bloodless" corpse of the drowned sailor, "a botch of reds and whites," is retrieved only to be cast back into the sea, the source of all creation. The theme of Part I is the horror and finality of death when viewed by those who have no belief in immortality. There is no hope for Warren Winslow and his fellow sailors in this nightmare vision: when the corpse is pitched out to sea, "dreadnaughts shall confess / Its hell-bent deity." As materialists, these sailors must reckon with the pagan deity Poseidon, the "earth-shaker," the cruel sea god. For them, death is final and irrevocable: "ask for no Orphean lute / To pluck life back."

The imagery of violence and destruction that pervades Part I is not modulated or significantly altered in subsequent sections, and the structural problem of the elegy is that Lowell does not quite seem to know where to go next. There is very little development in the first five sections. What happens, briefly stated, is that the poet shifts from the opening vision of contemporary wartime destruction to its historical counterpart, the meaningless voyage of Ahab's *Pequod*. The World War II battleship and the *Pequod* are explicitly linked in Part II, and the sinful pride of the Quak-

ers of Nantucket is related in Part III to the same sin as it
manifests itself in modern warfare. These sins are further
specified in II and III as being sins against Christ (the "hurt
beast," "IS, the whited monster"), and Part IV is, as Mazzaro
observes, a kind of dirge for Christianity, which has been
"killed" by the godlessness of Ahab's sailors and their modern counterparts (p. 39). Part V graphically describes the dis-
posal of the whale's rotting viscera, an act evidently symbolic
of the overwhelming evil that can be overcome only through
the intercession of Jonas Messias—Christ. The complicated
symbolism and rhetoric of these five sections mask a basic
confusion: if the *Pequod* was, in fact, sent "packing off to
hell" (IV), and if the figure of Warren Winslow merges with
Ahab's mariners, why will Christ intercede for him? What,
in other words, is the progress from sin to salvation?

Part VI, an adaptation of the description of Our Lady of
Walsingham in E. I. Watkin's *Catholic Art and Culture*,[26]
does not answer these questions, and its function in the
poem is puzzling. In an idyllic rural English setting, barefoot penitents are seen, walking along "the munching English lane," beside a gently flowing stream, and the speaker
tells Warren Winslow, "Sailor you were glad / and whistled
Sion by that stream." But the image of the Virgin herself
does not fulfill the sailor's expectations:

> There's no comeliness
> At all or charm in that expressionless
> Face with its heavy eyelids. As before,
> This face, for centuries a memory,
> *Non est species, neque decor,*
> Expressionless, expresses God.   [13]

Most commentators have praised the affirmation of this
passage, in which the familiar, materialistic salvation to
which a Warren Winslow might aspire ("castled Sion") is rejected in favor of a loftier vision of the universal but inscru-

table God who transcends all petty human concerns and aspirations. Mary's "expressionless" face paradoxically "Expresses God" in that it points to a knowledge lying beyond man's merely human desire to know.[27]

Although "Our Lady of Walsingham" is meant to provide the positive alternative to the sins the poet has been denouncing so vehemently, it fails to cohere with the rest of the poem. It is curious that those critics who have praised Lowell's perceptive handling of the American scene in "The Quaker Graveyard" have failed to ask why the locale of Part VI should be Walsingham. What does the English shrine in its pastoral setting have to do with the precarious existence of the Quakers in Nantucket? How shall the "world . . . come to Walsingham" when Lowell's world of S-boats and whalers has rejected Christianity? More specifically, if the "Sailor" (Warren Winslow) is made "glad" by the conventional description of heaven presented in the first stanza of VI, he is evidently incapable of understanding the significance of the face that "goes / Past castled Sion," just as Grandfather Winslow was incapable of hearing the *resurrexit dominus* and opted for a "painted Paradise of harps and lutes." In this case, the consolation can lie only in the speaker's superior vision of God; the sailor who is memorialized in the elegy is beyond redemption. The result is a certain smugness; it is as if the speaker were saying, "*I* know that 'She knows what God knows,' whereas ordinary men like my deceased cousin are satisfied with their limited vision of paradise." [28]

Within the larger context of the whole elegy, the shrine of Our Lady of Walsingham stands in sharp opposition to the Quaker Graveyard in Nantucket, and it is hard to see how these two symbolic locales can be fused. Again, to use Blackmur's phrase, there is "not a tension but a gritting." Part VII is therefore a rather lame conclusion. Richard Fein insists that VII is a "reaffirmation of God's covenant with man that despite man's dying in the sea . . . God's will remains above destruction," [29] and Mazzaro writes, "The poet having achieved the harmony of mystical union and its vision, Part VII reexamines the world without the sinister effects of the earlier sections" (p. 42). Granted the speaker says, "It's well" that the Atlantic is "fouled with blue sailors / Sea-monsters, upward angel, downward fish," [30] but the "empty winds" are still "creaking," the "greased wash" is still "exploding on a shoal-bell," and the act that the poet finally associates with the "time / When the Lord God formed man from the sea's slime" is the destructive movement of "blue-lung'd combers" that have "lumbered to the kill." The final affirmation, "The Lord survives the rainbow of His will," impressive as it is in itself, thus seems rather forced. It has not been implicit all along, as Milton's consolation has; even in the concluding section of the elegy, Lowell seems preoccupied with violence and destruction. It is as if the poet took one section of "Lycidas," the so-called digression in which Milton attacks the clergy (lines 109–31), and made this angry attack the substance of his vision. One remembers "The Quaker Graveyard" for its merciless invective against man-made violence and horror, a horror never really transcended within the limits of the elegy. For Warren Winslow, "dead at sea," the Virgin's "expressionless / Face with its heavy eyelids" is beyond reach: it expresses nothing at all. As for the poet himself, he never really comes to terms with the meaning of death as does the "I" of "Lycidas"; he may understand that the "expressionless" face "expresses God," but he cannot *relate* that expression to anything or anyone in his environment. He knows only that the dead who inhabit the Quaker Graveyard in Nantucket are eternally damned. Again the tone of the elegy belies its intended theme.

"My Last Afternoon with Uncle Devereux Winslow"

No one would compare "My Last Afternoon with Uncle Devereux Winslow," which appeared in *Life Studies* in 1959, to "Lycidas"; gone are the classical, historical, and

Biblical allusions, the complex liturgical symbolism, the oracular tone, the tight canzone form.[31] Like the earlier "In Memory of Arthur Winslow," this elegy is divided into four parts, but its development is entirely different: there is no progression from sickness, to burial scene, to "lament" for the dead man, to a prayer for his salvation. Part I characterizes Grandfather Winslow's summer home as it appeared to the narrator as a small boy, and the central character is Arthur Winslow himself, no longer the ruthless, godless capitalist of the earlier elegy, but a kindly if misguided man who has tried to place his individual stamp on his environment. Part II is a brief vignette in which Lowell depicts the boy's image of himself. Part III abruptly shifts to Grandmother Winslow's sister, Great Aunt Sarah, a lonely and aimless spinster who spends her days practicing for the concert she is never to give. Only in Part IV does Uncle Devereux, the boy's romantic hero, appear, and his premature death is related. The elegy ends on a note of death. There is no explicit consolation, no stated hope that the soul of Uncle Devereux will be saved.

Nevertheless, "My Last Afternoon with Uncle Devereux Winslow" is much more coherent, if less outwardly ambitious, than Lowell's earlier elegies. Hugh Staples has shown that the seemingly random observations of the narrator are carefully integrated by a pattern of imagery based on the elements of earth, water and air. "In Part I, the basic image is that of earth and the minerals that compose it. . . . The mineral images . . . though they suggest the wished-for permanence, are themselves mutable. Lifeless, they stand opposed to the world of human experience" (p. 79).

This very just observation deserves further development. The elegy's epigraph, "1922: the stone porch of my Grandfather's summer house," provides a key to the whole poem. The connotations of "stone porch"—lifelessness, the grave, death—immediately reverse those of "summer house"—

youth, warmth, vitality, life. The whole poem moves between these two poles, and yet, as the syntax of the epigraph makes clear, these opposites are found in conjunction; it is the "summer house" that has the "stone porch." Thus, unlike "In Memory of Arthur Winslow," this elegy does not set up a simple contrast between good and evil, salvation and sin; here it is difficult to extricate one from the other. Lowell manages to avoid the "gritting" or clash of opposites found in the earlier poem by a careful manipulation of tone. The mature narrator may well understand the futility of the lives of the Winslows, but for the young boy, his former self, "Nowhere was anywhere after a summer / at my Grandfather's farm." Moreover, "stone porch" and "summer house" are introduced at the very outset of the poem so that Lowell here avoids the jarring effect of Part VI of "The Quaker Graveyard," in which the religious consolation, totally unanticipated, is suddenly introduced.

The seemingly casual opening sets up the structural pattern:

"I won't go with you. I want to stay with Grandpa!
That's how I threw cold water
on my Mother and Father's
watery martini pipe dreams at Sunday dinner.   [*LS*, 59]

The "cold water" of line 2 becomes the poem's controlling image: it is the water of salvation, although here salvation has only a human, not a supernatural dimension. For the narrator's parents, "cold water" is an alien element; they have only "watery martini pipe dreams." The whole farm is characterized by a lack of water; even the poplar trees are "Diamond-pointed, athirst," and they "parade" unhappily "from Grandmother's rose garden" to "a scarey stand of virgin pine, / scrub, and paths forever pioneering." Throughout Part I, images of earth and water are carefully juxtaposed: Grandfather Winslow's "disproportioned" world is one of "Alpine Edwardian" cuckoo clocks, "slung with strangled, wooden game," of "fool's-gold nuggets," "octagonal red tiles, / sweaty with a secret dank, crummy with ant-stale." But when the maids Sadie and Nellie appear at sunset, "bearing pitchers of ice-tea, / oranges, lemons, mint and peppermints," they remind the boy who watches them from the stone porch of "sunflowers" and "Pumpkins floating shoulder-high." For the child, such moments are enough to prove that "Nowhere was anywhere after a summer / at my Grandfather's farm," but the narrator sees the inherent futility of the Edwardian elegance:

> The farm, entitled *Char-de-sa*
> in the Social Register,
> was named for my Grandfather's children:
> Charlotte, Devereux, and Sarah.   [*LS*, 60]

Not only does the silly, pretentious name *Char-de-sa* seem comically inappropriate for a farm, but the off-rhyme "Char-de-*sa*" / "Social Regist*er*" intensifies the hollowness of Winslow *moeurs contemporains*. (The same effect is created in Part III, where the meaningless round of Aunt Sarah's activities is summed up by off-rhyme in the lines, "Aunt Sarah, risen like a phoen*ix* / from her bed of troublesome sn*acks* and Tauchn*itz* class*ics*.") Part I ends on a note of death as the narrator recalls the demise of "Cinder, our Scottie puppy" ("Cinder" is again a mineral image) and sits "mixing black earth and lime," the two substances that will "blend to the one color" as an emblem of Uncle Devereux's death at the end of the elegy.

Part II presents the death-life paradox in terms of the boy's vision of himself in the mirror. The perfection of his "formal pearl gray shorts" (again a mineral image) gives the boy an illusion of permanence: he feels that he has "the Olympian / poise of my models in the imperishable autumn /

display windows / of Rogers Peet's boys' store." As he studies his reflection in the mirror, however, "Distorting drops of water / pinpricked my face." Life is not the false stasis of the shop window mannequin; it is flux, change, movement. The reality must be faced even if it is unpleasant: "I was a stuffed toucan / with a bibulous multicolored beak."

The seemingly random shift to Aunt Sarah in Part III presents a new variation on the same theme. Aunt Sarah's station is indoors, this side of the "lake-view window in the billiards-room"; she places a wall between herself and the water. The only event that can make her "rise like a phoenix" from her neurotic invalid's bed is the command of her sister, who, needing "a fourth for 'Auction,' " casts "a thirsty eye / On Aunt Sarah." The stone motif recurs in the image of the "naked Greek statues" that adorn Symphony Hall, "deathlike in the off-season summer," where Aunt Sarah formerly practiced on her soundless piano for her mythical recital.

The account of the actual physical death of Uncle Devereux, which is the subject of Part IV, jolts the reader with a sudden shock of recognition: it is only now that one realizes that all along the poem has been talking about death, the life-in-death of all the Winslows, whose carefully accumulated possessions are as ephemeral as the proper clothes, clever student poster, and "Double-barrelled shotguns" of Uncle Devereux, who is "dying of the incurable Hodgkin's disease." Again, Part IV opens with a water image:

> I picked with a clean finger nail at the blue anchor
> on my sailor blouse washed white as a spinnaker.
> What in the world was I wishing?
> . . . A sail-colored horse browsing in the bullrushes . . .
> A fluff of the west wind puffing
> my blouse, kiting me over our seven chimneys,
> troubling the water. . . .   [Spaced dots, Lowell's]

It is a lovely daydream, an escape into a world of water, whiteness and wind, but the reality rapidly intrudes with the ironic lines, "As small as sapphires were the ponds: *Quittacus, Snippituit* / and *Assawompset.*" Not only are the long Indian names of the little ponds amusingly pretentious; more significant is the fact that in Uncle Devereux's world it is difficult to distinguish life from death: water and mineral images merge—ponds become sapphires. Uncle Devereux is, in more than one sense, "closing camp for the winter":

> At the cabin between the waters,
> the nearest windows were already boarded.

The "cabin between the waters" is a key phrase in the elegy; the Winslow world is itself a "cabin between the waters," a lifeless entity surrounded by, but not participating in, the waters of life.

The description of the "disproportioned" world of Grandfather Winslow's stone porch in Part I has prepared us for the "helter-skelter" of Uncle Devereux's cabin where everything is incongruous, beginning with his attire, inappropriate for a sportsman, in "his severe / war-uniform of a volunteer Canadian officer." The only person whose thirst is quenched here is "Mr. Punch," grotesquely depicted as "a water melon in hockey tights," "tossing off a decanter of Scotch." The other posters similarly reflect the lack of direction in Uncle Devereux's life: "*La Belle France* in a red, white and blue toga / was accepting the arm of her 'protector,' / the ingenu and porcine Edward VII," and the narrator concludes sardonically:

> The finest poster was two or three young men in khaki
>   kilts
> being bushwhacked on the veldt—
> They were almost life-size. . . .
>   [*LS*, 63; spaced dots, Lowell's]

This terrible death of young men who are "almost life-size" prefigures Uncle Devereux's own death, explicitly

referred to in the next line. The poignancy of the closing
verse paragraph resides in the ironic contrast between the
Winslows' illusion that one can live forever and the reality
of death. Lovingly, year in and year out, Grandfather Winslow has "pencilled" "the white measuring-door" with Uncle
Devereux's heights until his son reached the eminence of six
feet in 1911. To the very end, Devereux maintains the illusion of "Olympian perfection" (Part II); he is, in the eyes of
the young boy, a figure of superhuman strength and splen-
dor: "His blue coat and white trousers / grew sharper and
straighter. / His coat was a blue jay's tail, / his trousers were
solid cream from the top of the bottle. / He was animated,
hierarchical." It is a splendid image but ultimately just as
lifeless as the "naked Greek statues" in Symphony Hall:
Uncle Devereux is no more than a "ginger snap man in a
clothes-press"—one wrong movement and he will break in
two. The black pile of earth and the white pile of lime will
"blend to the one color."

The final verse paragraph of the poem contains the only
passage in the elegy reminiscent of Lowell's earlier allusive
technique. In recording his reaction to the pointless argu-
ments between Grandfather Winslow and the dying Devereux, the speaker remembers:

> I cowered in terror.
> I wasn't a child at all—
> unseen and all-seeing, I was Agrippina
> in the Golden House of Nero.

What Lowell evidently means by the classical reference is
that, just as Agrippina "cowered in terror" after her son
Brittanicus was poisoned and, fearing for her safety, spied on
her treacherous son Nero behind palace doors, so the child,
"unseen and all-seeing," makes an unconscious connection
between the death of others—in this case Devereux—and
his own annihilation. Again, like Agrippina, the speaker in
Lowell's elegy has to maintain the aristocratic tradition in

the face of a decadent world. The fall of his house symbolizes the fall of a larger social order.[32]

But such explication does not take us very far. If one con-
siders the function rather than the source of the passage, it
becomes readily apparent that the lines are out of key with
the rest of the elegy. The tone throughout has been one of
quiet understatement, of ironic implication; the narrator has
kept his eye squarely on the objects that surround him and
has read their lesson obliquely. In the structure created by
the contrasting earth and water images, the sudden reference
to Agrippina seems strained and overy explicit. We do not
need to be told that the speaker "wasn't a child at all," for
the poem has already dramatized the intensity of the child's
vision, and the insistence on his "all-seeing" power seems labored and sentimental. It is the only time that tone falters in
this otherwise superbly articulated poem.

As an elegy, "My Last Afternoon with Uncle Devereux
Winslow" stands at the opposite pole from "In Memory of
Arthur Winslow" and "The Quaker Graveyard." In the
early elegies, the death of the relative was used as a mere
starting point for a satiric attack on the evils of contemporary civilization. "Uncle Devereux Winslow," outwardly so
unlike a classical elegy like "Lycidas," is actually closer to it
than is "The Quaker Graveyard," for the later elegy does
contain the lament for the premature death of the young
man which is a basic requirement of the elegy form. Because
we see Devereux both from the angle of vision of the child
and from that of the mature narrator recalling his childhood, we can sympathize with the dying man who is the
boy's hero, even as we judge him. "Uncle Devereux Winslow" also contains, if only implicitly, the consolation motif
essential to elegy: the poet speaker, in the act of recalling his
childhood, has learned that only by accepting the lives of
others can one go beyond them. The central theme of the
poem—the need to accept the flux of life, to "throw cold

water" on one's "watery martini pipe dreams," to leave "the cabin between the waters"—is surely one that transcends the local concerns of the Lowell-Winslow family. Despite its autobiographical emphasis, "Uncle Devereux Winslow" is paradoxically a less private and more universal poem than the two earlier elegies which strain unsuccessfully to make the death of one man symbolic of the death of the whole New England tradition.

"Soft Wood"

The title of Lowell's next volume of poetry, *For the Union Dead* (1964), reveals the poet's continuing concern with the problem of mortality. But after the intense concentration on his family in *Life Studies,* Lowell now turns to more public subjects, and the title poem is a brilliant generalized lament in the tradition of Gray's "Elegy in a Country Churchyard." The collection does, however, contain one Winslow elegy, "Soft Wood," written in memory of the poet's cousin Harriet Winslow. Compared to, say, "The Quaker Graveyard," this looks like a slight, unimposing lyric, but its offhand casualness turns out to be a carefully calculated effect.

"Soft Wood" (*FUD*, 63–64) is curiously reminiscent of Yeats's "The Wild Swans at Coole": in both poems, the central thematic antithesis is between the eternal renewal or immortality of nature and the mortality of man. Observing the swans, Yeats's speaker asks, "Among what rushes will they build, / By what lake's edge or pool / Delight men's eyes when I awake some day / To find they have flown away?" Just so, Lowell's lament for mortality in Stanza VI is followed by the statement, "Yet the seal pack will bark past my window / summer after summer." Even the six-line stanza of "Soft Wood" resembles that of "The Wild Swans at Coole," although the stress pattern is different, and Lowell does not use a regular rhyme scheme as does Yeats.[33]

Matthew Arnold's "The Scholar-Gypsy," which provided Lowell with the stanza form for "In Memory of Arthur Winslow," here furnishes him his witty opening metaphor: the seals, happily swimming "in their barred pond at the zoo," oddly remind the speaker of the mysterious Oxford boy who disappeared from the university in the remote past, became a gypsy, and returned to haunt students of subsequent generations. In Arnold's poem, the scholar-gypsy becomes the symbol for the free, instinctive, natural life, unencumbered by the normal man's "sick fatigue," "Languid doubt," "heads o'ertax'd," and "palsied hearts"; similarly, Lowell's seals, which pop up suddenly on the surface of the water and then unexpectedly disappear again, symbolize the instinctive and irrational element in life.

The seals are "happy" because they are at home in nature, just as Yeats's swans find the cold streams "Companionable." The lines "and no sunflower turns / more delicately to the sun / without a wincing of the will," recall Yeats's lines, "Passion or conquest, wander where they will / Attend upon them still." The natural world is the seals' habitat and so there is no need for a "wincing of the will."

Stanza II opens with the line "Here too in Maine things bend to the wind forever." "Too" is a puzzling word; it implies that "things" should "bend to the wind forever" even as the sunflower turns to the sun. The rest of the stanza bears out this implication. Along the Maine coast, one has the illusion of being able to live forever—the "painted soft wood" of the oceanfront houses stays "bright and clean" indefinitely as the air blasts "an all-white wall whiter," and the wind, tinged with the aroma of salt and evergreen, is a welcome force. But it is already clear that the difference between seal pond and Maine seaport is that in the latter eternal life is only an illusion—"to bend to the wind" is ultimately to die.

The illusion persists in the next stanza, in which wind imagery is replaced by that of water: "The green juniper berry spills crystal-clear gin, / and even the hot water in the bath-tub / is more than water, / and rich with the scouring effer-vescence / of something healing, / the illimitable salt." This magically healing water recalls the water imagery of "Uncle Devereux Winslow": it is the water of life, health, salvation. But the positive emphasis is undercut by the contrast be-tween this water and the pond the seals swim in. Water is not man's natural habitat—he must crush the juniper berry in order to extract the flavoring for the "crystal-clear gin," and the "hot water in the bathtub" is, after all, a man-made product.

Not surprisingly, therefore, a note of doubt enters in the fourth stanza. "Things last," the narrator says cryptically, but the wind that formerly blew "through curtain and screen / touched with salt and evergreen," now becomes, in a transformation that recalls the poems of Wallace Stevens, "the wind smashing without direction." The ceaseless mo-notony of the air blast reduces the mind to nothingness so that man forgets his responsibilities: "only children seem fit to handle children." And even the "fresh paint on the cap-tains' houses" cannot hide the fact that the wood is becom-ing "softer."

The whitening action of the wind upon "Soft Wood" re-calls another image to the narrator's mind in Stanza VII: the dazzling display of power in the days when the captains' "square-riggers used to whiten / the four corners of the globe." But their command of the ocean was, again, short-lived and illusory: the captains hardly "outlast their posses-sions, / once warped and mothered by their touch." Not only is the acquisition of "things" that supposedly "last" use-less, but in the stanza's final line, the human body itself is seen as a thing, as one more useless possession:

Shed skin will never fit another wearer.

This ominously quiet line with its feminine endings ("nev*er*," "anoth*er*," wear*er*") suddenly forces the reader into

an awareness that all along it has been death, not life, that
has been the subject of the poet's meditation. It is the same
effect that Lowell created in Part IV of "Uncle Devereux
Winslow," but in "Soft Wood" the poet achieves it with
greater economy.

The phrase "shed skin" reminds one of the seals (sealskin),
to whom the poet now returns. "Shed skin" is no problem in
the seal world, for new seals "will bark past" the poet's window "summer after summer." But for human beings, especially for the aged, it is different. "This is the season / when
our friends may and will die daily. / Surely the lives of the
old / are briefer than the young." Just as the wood seems to
be eternally white, so the young seem to be immortal; "the
lives of the old / are briefer," because not a day goes by
without a reminder that someone old has died.

Only now, in the last stanza, does Lowell attack the subject of the elegy directly: "Harriet Winslow, who owned this
house, / was more to me than my mother." One can accept
the flat statement of these lines because Lowell has already
dramatized Harriet Winslow's world, in which the "juniper
berry spills crystal-clear gin" and "even the hot water in the
bathtub" has a "scouring effervescence." As the embodiment
of that world, Harriet Winslow seemed immortal to her
younger cousin; the truth that she has "bent to the wind" is
almost impossible to grasp. The distance between the
speaker and the lamented dead is measured in the last three
lines of the elegy by the symbolic distance between Washington, city of heat waves and air-conditioning, and Maine, with
its whiteness, water, wind, and evergreen. "Breathing in the
heat wave" is the opposite of breathing the fresh air that
"blows through curtain and screen" of Harriet Winslow's
house; the heat waves of Washington also stand opposed to
the ocean waves of Maine. The air-conditioning is thus a
drug that numbs—one forgets the heat, but simultaneously
its "air blast" alerts the poet to the painful recollection of an
air blast that was natural and enervating.

In "Soft Wood," lament and consolation come together in the climactic line, "Shed skin will never fit another wearer." The speaker laments the mortality of his beloved relative, but he knows that there is another level of awareness at which "shed skin" is no tragedy. The elegy's water imagery is functional here: the seals are at home in the water but, being mindless, they accept it "without a wincing of the will." Harriet Winslow, on the other hand, is a mere shore dweller; she is not at home in nature as are the seals, and the wind can become a terrifying sound in her mind; however, she and the poet who mourns for her can do what the seals cannot—they can see, assess, understand. "Knowing" is thus the crucial verb in the last stanza.

The problem of tonal irresolution of Lowell's early elegies —what Geoffrey Hartman aptly calls "an unfortunate grinding together of natural experience and supernatural emblem" [34]—is thus solved in "Soft Wood" because natural experience, the poet's awareness of Harriet Winslow's death, and supernatural emblem, the life-giving water of Maine, are closely related. As in the case of "Uncle Devereux Winslow," the balance between lament and consolation, between sympathy and judgment is carefully maintained.

"Fourth of July in Maine"

Lowell's second elegy for Harriet Winslow, "Fourth of July in Maine," which appeared in *Near the Ocean* in 1967, is representative of his more recent work.[35] The poem begins with a description of the annual Independence Day parade held on the morning of the Fourth and culminates in the nighttime fireside vigil of the poet and his wife in the house they have inherited from Harriet Winslow. In the course of the poem, the speaker pays tribute to his cousin as the embodiment of the traditional values of New England, now in decay, and prays that his daughter, named after Cousin Harriet, will inherit not only her house but also her sense of proportion, her gift for friendship, and her independence.

Such a summary makes "Fourth of July in Maine" sound rather like Yeats's "A Prayer for my Daughter" or his Coole Park poems, but whereas Yeats's "I" is passionately involved in the events and situations of which he speaks, the protagonist of Lowell's elegy seems to stand outside the experience of his fellow men, surveying their activities with the jaundiced eye of the stern and disenchanted witness. The "I" of "Soft Wood" is now replaced by a generalized and sometimes smug "we"—a reference to those of us who are in the know:

> Blue twinges of mortality
> remind us the theocracy
> drove in its stakes here to command
> the infinite.   [NO, 28]

Even the verse form—the octosyllabic couplet—relates "Fourth of July in Maine" to a Restoration satire like "Hudibras" rather than to the meditative elegiac poem.

"Fourth of July in Maine" cannot, in fact, make up its mind whether it is primarily a satire or an elegy. The first four stanzas are clearly satiric; the Independence Day parade, "all innocence / of children's costumes," prompts the poet's denunciation of the false patriotism that blinds Americans to the truth that they are "world-losers everywhere" even if they are "conquerors here" (Stanza I), and his scorn for the blind conservatism of those Maine Republicans who, as "scions of the good old strain," accept their poverty as a *fait accompli,* combining "Emersonian self-reliance" with the "lethargy of Russian peasants" (Stanza II). Under these circumstances, the statue of the Union Soldier, the representative of a more heroic past, can only be "elbowed off the stage, / while the canned martial music fades." The poet places the blame for such debasement of the American dream squarely on the shoulders of the Puritan theocracy, "a ministry that would have made / short work of Christ, the Son of God, /

and then exchanged His crucifix, / hardly our sign, for politics" (*NO*, 28).

The nonchalance and casual speech of this passage should not obscure the realization that the poet has taken us back full circle to the world of *Lord Weary's Castle*. He is still quarreling with his Puritan ancestors, deriding the power-hungry Puritan theocracy and blaming the nation's current malaise on the original "dark design / spun by God and Cotton Mather" (29). Addressing New England directly, he warns his community that its *"bel età dell' oro"* is really "thinner than a cobweb, / caught in Calvinism's web."

In delivering this quasi-sermon, the poet has all but forgotten Harriet Winslow and her house. Accordingly, when he declares in Stanza V that "This white Colonial frame house, / willed downward, Dear, from you to us, / still matters," the reader is puzzled. How can a Colonial frame house *matter* in these dark days when even the Union Soldier is "elbowed off the stage"?

The problem is not resolved in the middle portion of the poem (Stanzas VII–XI), which memorializes Harriet Winslow. Although Lowell no longer views his relatives in terms of their ultimate salvation or damnation, his treatment of his cousin is less affectionate than it is patronizing and even slightly malicious. The first thing one learns about Cousin Harriet is that she has already been forgotten by all: "Dear Cousin, life is much the same, / though only fossils know your name / here since you left this solitude." Harriet's lack of renown is hardly surprising, the poem implies, for she was a person entirely without distinction. Her two ruling passions were gossip and interior decorating:

> If memory is genius, you
> had Homer's, enough gossip to
> repeople Trollope's Barchester,
> nurses, Negro, diplomat, down-easter,
> cousins kept up with, nipped, corrected,
> kindly, majorfully directed,

>   though family furniture, decor.
>   and rooms redone meant almost more.   [*NO, 30*]

Cousin Harriet is, in short, memorialized as a rather prying busybody, who felt called upon to *nip, correct,* and *direct* her friends, relatives, and servants; a woman who reserved her real affection for old furniture. Even after she had suffered a paralyzing stroke, she drew mental inventories of the objects in the rooms she could no longer visit or redecorate (Stanza IX). Her musical interests, moreover, are singled out for gentle ridicule by the poet:

>   High New England summer, warm
>   and fortified against the storm
>   by nightly nips you once adored,
>   though never going overboard,
>   Harriet, when you used to play
>   your chosen Nadia Boulanger
>   Monteverdi, Purcell, and Bach's
>   precursors on the Magnavox.   [*NO, 31*]

A proper lady, Harriet adores her "nightly nips" but knows when to stop. "Fortified against the storm," perhaps by a little sherry or brandy, she settles down to "play," not a musical instrument, but the recordings made by a very different lady, Nadia Boulanger, whose teaching inspired many great composers of the twentieth century. The off rhyme, "B*ach's*" / "Magna*vox*" has an ironically deflating effect; it underlines the essential passivity of Harriet Winslow's "culture" in which everything becomes grist for the mill and even Bach is finally eaten up alive by the Magnavox.

After this satiric portrait of Harriet Winslow, the prayer for the poet's daughter in Stanza XI can hardly be taken very seriously. Can the poet really hope that:

>   may your proportion strengthen her
>   to live through the millennial year
>   Two Thousand, and like you possess
>   friends, independence, and a house.

"Friends" in the context of the preceding stanzas can only mean people whom one *nips* and *corrects*—in short, whom one manipulates. "Independence" means the wealth to ignore the poor of Stanza II who "will not sink and cannot swim." "Proportion" can refer to nothing much more significant than remembering not to take that second drink when one is getting ready to listen to Purcell. Even the white frame house seems to be a useless legacy, for the poem has made clear that it is no refuge from the absurdities and atrocities existing beyond its doors. The future, in fact, seems to belong to the little guinea pigs, his daughter's pets, who are characterized in Stanzas XII and XIII as "Man's poorest cousins, harmonies / of lust and appetite and ease. . . . Evolution's snails by birth, / outrunning man who runs the earth."

It is curious that only in the last four stanzas of "Fourth of July in Maine," when Lowell finally drops both the satiric mask and the tribute to the dead relative, does the poem recapture the authenticity and intensity of "Uncle Devereux Winslow" or "Soft Wood." As the evening of this Independence Day becomes darker, the poet's increasing personal anguish and anxiety is reflected in images of dislocation and distortion:

> And now the frosted summer night-dew
> brightens, the north wind rushes through
> your ailing cedars, finds the gaps;
> thumbtacks rattle from the white maps,
> food's lost sight of, dinner waits,
> in the cold oven, icy plates—
> repeating and repeating, one
> Joan Baez on the gramophone.   [*NO*, 33]

The moment recorded is one of total emptiness: the rattling of thumbtacks holding up maps that have neither shapes nor colors on their oddly blank surfaces, and the monotonously repetitive replay of Joan Baez's voice on the

Magnavox succeed in reducing the self to an empty shell. All desire to eat dinner—or indeed to make any decision—evaporates, and the cold oven and icy plates reflect the speaker's inner temperature.

Staring blankly at the fire, the poet vaguely regrets a time when man "still licensed to increase, / unfallen and un-mated, heard / only the uncreated Word." But innocence is no longer possible in this world in which the Logos has been replaced by the logs, burning to nothing in the fireplace. The poet's real prayer is not for his daughter and has noth-ing to do with Harriet Winslow; it is a prayer for himself:

> Great ash and sun of freedom, give
> us this day the warmth to live,
> and face the household fire.   [NO, 34]

But he knows that his is not the grand gesture or the heroic act. Fatigued and cowardly, he gives up the challenge and so, "We turn / our backs, and feel the whiskey burn."

If the ending of "Fourth of July in Maine" seems so much more effective than the rest of the poem, it is surely because here the poet turns inward, assessing his own impulses and behavior with the same irony, pathos, and candor one finds in "91 Revere Street" and the *Life Studies* poems. Like Yeats, Lowell is at his best when he can make a drama out of his own life, when his "I," rooted firmly in time and space, undergoes a particular experience which leads to illumina-tion and insight. As a satirist, Lowell ultimately fails because he is uncertain of both his object of attack and the norm against which that object must be measured. Harriet Wins-low cannot be taken seriously as the subject of the elegy be-cause she is characterized as being precisely like those Maine Republicans, those self-reliant, self-assertive, patriotic New Englanders whom Lowell attacks in the first section of the poem. She represents, in other words, no clearly definable set of values that can be set over against the values of the Independence Day marchers. Therefore, despite the references to "Dear Cousin" or "your tireless sedentary love," Lowell's praise of Harriet Winslow can only sound half-hearted, and the poet's prayer for his daughter becomes a kind of parody-prayer. In "Soft Wood," Lowell circumvents the problem because the "I" is depicted in the process of learning to relate the death of one loved person to the larger life-death cycle of nature. Wisely, the poet does not dwell on Harriet Winslow's hobbies and interests in the earlier elegy; her role in "Soft Wood" is simply that of the generic beloved relative. "Fourth of July in Maine," however, confuses elegiac lament with satire and moves ultimately not toward a consolatory vision but toward fatigue.

In a particularly acute review of *Near the Ocean,* John Holloway has argued that in his later work, Lowell "wrestles uneasily with the public dimension." "There is an effort toward the public world, but . . . there is no mastery of it or assurance within it." [36] This is not to say that Lowell can only master what Holloway calls "private resonances." In his best poetry, the outside or public world is very much present, but it is viewed from the vantage point of the introspective, suffering self: one thinks of "Skunk Hour," of "Man and Wife," of "For the Union Dead," as well as of such Winslow elegies as "Uncle Devereux Winslow. It is only when the poet strains to make public pronouncements that will have objective validity—"the world shall come to Walsingham" or "Civil Rights clergy face again / the scions of the good old strain"—that the didactic impulse threatens to overcome the poetic. The voice that castigates the New England Puritanism of the Lowells and Winslows is that of a poet who still dwells in the shadow of his New England family tree.

Conclusion

Lowell and Some Contemporaries: A Portrait of the Artist as Mental Patient

In each of the preceding chapters, I have looked at Lowell's poetry from a partial perspective, examining in turn his structure of imagery (a structure whose very coherence and consistency make it difficult for the poet to be a good translator), his confessional mode, his syntax, and his struggle to create a viable lyric voice. We may now be in a position to tackle a more formidable problem: to define, in larger terms, Lowell's characteristic poetic style and to view that style against the background of contemporary poetry.

In his essay on Pasternak's early prose, Roman Jakobson has observed, "As in the games of the magicians, the hero is difficult to discern: he disintegrates into a series of elements and attributes; he is replaced by a network of externalizations of his own states of mind, and by the objects, animate or inanimate, that surround him. . . . what properly constitutes him as a hero—his activity—escapes our perception; action disappears behind topography." [1]

This would be an excellent description of the style of *Life Studies*. As I have suggested in earlier chapters, Lowell is essentially a post-Symbolist poet, whose characteristic mode is what we may call the "realistic" or "documentary" or "metonymic" lyric. The clotted and charged symbolist mode of *Lord Weary's Castle* and *The Mills of the Kavanaughs* soon gives way to a poetry at once highly personal and highly factual, a poetry that combines Wordsworthian confessionalism with a Chekhovian "totality of objects." [2] Jakobson's observation that "action disappears behind topography" is, in fact, oddly echoed by the poet's reflection in "Beyond the Alps" that "Life changed to landscape."

How has this particular lyric mode influenced contemporary poets? We may answer this difficult question, at least in part, by examining one of Lowell's widely known poems in *Life Studies,* "Waking in the Blue," and comparing it to some contemporary poems in precisely the same genre, a genre which we may call, for want of a better term, the *mental hospital poem.* Such comparison will, I believe, be especially helpful, for in seeing what Lowell's poetry is *not,* we may come to a clearer understanding of what it *is.*

Waking in the Blue

The night attendant, a B.U. sophomore,
rouses from the mare's nest of his drowsy head
propped on *The Meaning of Meaning.*
He catwalks down our corridor.
Azure day
makes my agonized blue window bleaker.
Crows maunder on the petrified fairway.
Absence! My heart grows tense
as though a harpoon were sparring for the kill.
(This is the house for the "mentally ill.")

What use is my sense of humor?
I grin at Stanley, now sunk in his sixties,
once a Harvard all-American fullback,
(if such were possible)
still hoarding the build of a boy in his twenties,
as he soaks, a ramrod
with the muscle of a seal
in his long tub,
vaguely urinous from the Victorian plumbing.

A kingly granite profile in a crimson golf-cap,
worn all day, all night,
he thinks only of his figure,
of slimming on sherbet and ginger ale—
more cut off from words than a seal.

This is the way day breaks in Bowditch Hall at McLean's;
the hooded night lights bring out "Bobbie,"
Porcellian '29,
a replica of Louis XVI
without the wig—
redolent and roly-poly as a sperm whale,
as he swashbuckles about in his birthday suit
and horses at chairs.

These victorious figures of bravado ossified young.

In between the limits of day,
hours and hours go by under the crew haircuts
and slightly too little nonsensical bachelor twinkle
of the Roman Catholic attendants.
(There are no Mayflower
screwballs in the Catholic Church.)

After a hearty New England breakfast,
I weigh two hundred pounds
this morning. Cock of the walk,
I strut in my turtle-necked French sailor's jersey
before the metal shaving mirrors,
and see the shaky future grow familiar
in the pinched, indigenous faces
of these thoroughbred mental cases,
twice my age and half my weight.
We are all old-timers,
each of us holds a locked razor.   [LS, 81–82]

Like "Man and Wife," discussed in Chapter Three, "Waking in the Blue" is a variant of what M. H. Abrams has called "the greater Romantic lyric," the autobiographical poem in which a determinate speaker—the "I" of the poet—carries on a "sustained colloquy" with himself. The speaker begins with a description of the outer scene: in this case, the bed-room-bathroom-corridor world of Bowditch Hall at fashionable McLean's Sanatorium outside Boston. Certain aspects of this scene, particularly the absurd and pathetic morning "physical fitness" rituals of Stanley and Bobbie, both former Harvard men, evoke in the poet what Abrams calls "a varied but integral process of memory, thought, anticipation, and feeling."[3] In the course of his meditation the poet moves toward the realization that, despite his original amused contempt for the antics of these "victorious figures of bravado," he is actually one of them. Aloofness ("What use is my sense of humor?") gradually gives way to empathy: the poet sees his own "shaky future" mirrored in the "pinched, indigenous faces / Of these thoroughbred mental cases, / twice my age and half my weight." The poem thus comes full circle, ending as it began with a description of the external scene —the shaving rite at the bathroom mirror—but with the speaker's deepened understanding that "We are all old-timers, / each of us holds a locked razor."

So much for the poem's basic mode. Within the relatively short space of its fifty lines, "Waking in the Blue" contains in microcosm the structure of imagery described in Chapter One. The world of nature, to begin with, is merely a reflection of the poet's anxiety: the advent of "Azure day," far from bringing the mental patient a sense of relief, only makes his "agonized blue window bleaker." The landscape itself has turned to metal and stone: like the crows who "maunder on the petrified fairway," the poet's fellow inmates have "ossified young." Thus Stanley, the former football star, has a "granite profile," and the world of the mental patients is circumscribed by metal shaving mirrors, locked razors, and imaginary harpoons about to strike. In this petrified landscape, men have been reduced to ludicrous animals.

Stanley may look like a "ramrod" but has no more than the "muscle of a seal"; "roly-poly" Bobbie is a parody version of a sperm-whale, and the poet, who fancies himself the "Cock of the walk," is comically reduced in status by the reference to his "*turtle*-necked . . . jersey."

In the poet's dormitory, significantly named "Bow*ditch* Hall," all is confused motion and decay. The "drowsy head" of the Boston University sophomore who acts as night attendant is a "mare's nest"; the crows "maunder," Bobbie "swashbuckles about in his birthday suit / and horses at chairs," the poet himself struts up to the shaving mirror only to dissolve in fear. The hospital window is "bleak," the night lights "hooded," and the bathtub in which Stanley soaks is "vaguely urinous from the Victorian plumbing." As so often in Lowell's poetry, feet fail to make contact with the earth and hands cannot reach one another: thus the attendant "catwalks down the corridor," and the only thing the poet and his fellow inmates hold is a "locked razor."

Not only is the poem's setting a mental hospital, but hospital and prison images—two of Lowell's most pervasive clusters—merge. The "B.U. sophomore", for example, treats the corridor as a catwalk, insulating himself from possible contact with the "thoroughbred mental cases" in his charge. The crows cannot depart from the petrified fairway, and Stanley, soaking in his tub, is "more cut off from words than a seal." The poet's own sense of confinement is repeatedly emphasized: his "agonized blue window" admits no fresh air from the world beyond the sanatorium; his razor is "locked." Indeed, time itself seems to be imprisoned here: "In between the limits of day," the hours constitute a meaningless vacuum, and there is no escape for the patient under the surveillance of the "crew haircuts / and slightly too little nonsensical twinkle" of the Roman Catholic attendants. The hospital-prison world, moreover, is perilously close to the graveyard. As soon as day breaks, the poet is overwhelmed by a sense of inner emptiness and the fear of death:

Absence! My heart grows tense
as though a harpoon were sparring for the kill.

Against this background of petrifaction and restriction, Lowell presents a cast of characters at once individual and typical. The basic tension in the poem is between "May-flower screwballs" and their Roman Catholic attendants, between a Boston Brahmin tradition gone sour and the new conformist Irish-Catholic bourgeoisie, between Harvard and Boston University. Lowell's juxtapositions here are almost Laingian; one wonders who is "saner": Stanley, the one-time athlete "now sunk in his sixties," who wears his crimson golf-cap to bed and "thinks only of his figure," or the sophomoric night attendant whose mind is so overwhelmed by the subtle semantics of Ogden and Richards that it has become a "mare's nest." Or again, who is more ridiculous: Bobbie, once a member of Harvard's elite Porcellian club, who looks like Louis XVI "without the wig" and "horses at chairs," or the solemn Catholic attendants with their "crew haircut" and no-nonsense "twinkle"? The poet himself identifies with Stanley and Bobbie: it is no coincidence that he eats "a hearty *New England* breakfast" and struts about like a proud cock. Like Stanley and Bobbie, he is a "thoroughbred"—of such pure and unmixed stock that he can, ironically, no longer cope with ordinary reality.

Time references play an important part in "Waking in the Blue." The poem begins with the coming of "Azure day"; it describes one typical morning in the life of the poet as mental patient at McLean's. But the past intrudes repeatedly: Stanley, *"now* sunk in his sixties," was *once* a Harvard fullback; Bobbie is "Porcellian '29"; most of the inmates are "twice my age and half my weight." The hours and hours that "go by" "in between the limits of day" may be a vacuum for the patients, but in the poet's imagination they are progressively charged with the past: what people are has meaning only in relation to what they have been. If the poet's

see 177

future is "shaky," it is because it is built on a past of crumbling sand. In this context, the key phrase is "We are all old-timers"—the old-timers on the hospital ward are ironically the most venerable old-timers America can offer: the heirs of the Pilgrims turned "Mayflower screwballs."

How are Lowell's images of person, place, and time, of decayed nature, disease, prison, and death related within the basically circular structure of "Waking in the Blue"? As in the case of the poems discussed in Chapters Three and Four, Lowell's central images are carefully arranged in a series of metonymic sequences. In the first stanza, for example, the poet is immediately decomposed into the chaotic and pointless activities and unpleasant objects that surround him. There are three main sequences here: the series of alliterating nouns and verbs, "*mare's nest," "Meaning of Meaning,"* and "*maunder,"* which defines the poet's peculiar disorientation and confusion; the sequence "catwalks," "corridor," and "petrified fairway," which looks ahead to "Cock of the walk" in the last stanza and emphasizes the overriding sense that the poet has lost his way; and the progression, underlined by the assonance of *a*'s, from "*Azure* day" to "*agonized blue window*" to "*Absence*," in which the blue sky is rapidly transformed into the void of outer space.

The passivity of the poet's world is further defined by the poem's syntax. In the opening sentence, for example, the subject-verb construction ("The night attendant . . . rouses") is immediately undercut by phrasal modification:

> The night attendant
>
> a B.U. sophomore
>
>   rouses from the mare's nest
>   ↑
>   of his drowsy head
>   ↑
>   propped on *The Meaning*
>   ↑
>   *of Meaning.*

Similarly, the recurrent past participles define the inertia of the hospital world: the attendant's "drowsy head" is *"propped* on *The Meaning of Meaning,"* the "blue window" is *"agonized,"* the fairway *"petrified."* This pattern continues to operate throughout the poem: Stanley is *"sunk* in his sixties," his cap is *"worn* all day, all night," the "night lights" are *"hooded,"* the faces *"pinched."*

In the middle stanzas of the poem, Lowell continues to present his "I" indirectly; the speaker is now reflected in the physical appearance of his companions, Stanley and Bobbie. Syntactically, both characters are again subordinated to their attributes, as in the following lines in which a long noun phrase in apposition precedes the subject pronoun:

> A kingly granite profile in a crimson golf-cap
>
>   worn all day, all night,
>
> he thinks. . . .

Recurrent references to body size and weight unify this portion of "Waking in the Blue" and relate it to the final stanzas. Thus the poem moves from Stanley's incongruous appearance as a "ramrod / with the muscle of a seal," to Bobbie's flabby corpulence ("redolent and roly-poly"), to the poet's own weight ("two-hundred pounds"), a weight that links him directly to those other "victorious figures of bravado" who have "ossified young." His physical fitness is as illusory as theirs, his future equally "shaky"—a word that harks back to "catwalks," "maunder," "swashbuckles," "horses," and "twinkle."

"Waking in the Blue" concludes with the emblem of the "locked razor," an image that has been anticipated not only by such mineral images as the "petrified fairway," Stanley's "granite profile," and the "metal shaving mirrors," but also by the imaginary harpoon "sparring for the kill" of line 9. In civilized society, the poem implies, the harpoon may well be obsolete, but the locked razor can be just as deadly.

"Waking in the Blue," after all, suggests an awakening or transition not to life but to death.

Despite its painful theme, this is a poem remarkably free of self-pity. Here prosody surely plays a part. If we look at the first stanza of "Waking in the Blue," for example, we may note that although six of its ten lines have ten or eleven syllables, the effect is not that of iambic pentameter. Rather, these lines tend to have four main stresses. This may well be the case because, as Lowell explains in the *Paris Review* interview, many of the *Life Studies* poems were begun in "perfectly strict four-foot couplets" and loosened up by adding articles and prepositions. There is the ghost of such a couplet in the stanza's final lines:

> as though a harpoon were sparring for the kill.
> (This is the house for the "mentally ill.")

"It was a great help," Lowell says with reference to "Commander Lowell," "when I was revising to have this original skeleton. I could keep the couplets where I wanted them and drop them where I didn't; there'd be a form to come back to." [4]

Thus, whereas Pound's free verse, for example, is characterized by clusters of heavy stresses falling on long vowels, Lowell tends to stress very lightly, creating the effect of casual conversation, of understatement:

> I grin at Stanley, now sunk in his sixties
>
> as he swashbuckles about in his birthday suit

Another characteristic of Lowell's prosody is that the rhythm is generally falling:

> propped on *The Meaning of Meaning*

vaguely urinous from the Victorian plumbing

After a hearty New England breakfast

The combination of light stressing and falling rhythm gives Lowell's poetry its peculiarly tentative quality: the speaker's voice falters as he repeatedly uses feminine endings:

What use is my sense of *humor?*

sunk in his *sixties*

still *hoarding* the build of a boy in his *twenties*

Yet Lowell avoids prosaic flatness by using highly intricate and artful qualitative sound patterns. Note, for example, the use of assonance, alliteration, rhyme, and repetition in the first stanza:

The night attendant, a B.U. sophomore,
rouses from the mare's nest of his drowsy head
propped on *The Meaning of Meaning.*
He catwalks down our corridor.
Azure day
makes my agonized blue window bleaker.
Crows maunder on the petrified fairway.
Absence! My heart grows tense
as though a harpoon were sparring for the kill.
(This is the house for the "mentally ill.") [5]

Lowell's verse is, in fact, highly structured, but the effects are muted because the rhymes are frequently buried, as in "sophom*ore*" / "corri*dor*," "r*ouses*" / "dr*ow*sy," and *"har-*

poon" / "s*par*ring," while assonantal patterns are offset by harsh consonants, as in lines 5–6, where chiastic assonance is played off against voiced and voiceless stops:

Azure day
[*1*]   [*2*]
ma<u>k</u>es my a<u>g</u>onize<u>d</u> <u>b</u>lue win<u>d</u>ow <u>b</u>lea<u>k</u>er.
[*2*]   [*1*]

Such sound patterning helps to give Lowell's free verse its tone of calculated ease; it screens the reader from what would be the excessive pathos of the situation described in the poem. Throughout "Waking in the Blue," moreover, the self is distanced and presented in all its essential incongruity and absurdity: the poet can "grin" not only at Stanley, Bobbie, and the Roman Catholic attendants but also at himself. He is not, for example, above eating a "hearty New England breakfast," caring about the way he looks in his "French sailor's jersey," or lording it over the hospital's old-timers. His suffering is thus presented less as a matter of personal pathology than as a microcosm of our solipsistic, self-indulgent *angst*. The speaker's initial question—"What good is my sense of humor?"—is ultimately answered by the poem itself.

In Chapter Three, I suggested that *Life Studies* marked a turning point in the history of modern poetry, and indeed "Waking in the Blue" has given birth to a whole line of "hospital poems," superficially like Lowell's in their stress on personal suffering, precise disease and hospital imagery, documentary veracity in the treatment of persons and places, and a tone that can accommodate both to the horror and the humor of the patient's situation. Most of the poems in Anne Sexton's *To Bedlam and Part of the Way Back* [1960] are written on the Lowell model, as are many of Berryman's *Dream Songs* of the early sixties: for example, "Room 231:

the fourth week" [#92] and "Ill lay he long, upon this last return" [#94]. Among more recent poems, we may cite Christopher Middleton's "The Ballad of the Psychoanalyst" from *Cairns* [1969], James Dickey's "Diabetes" and "The Cancer Match," both of which appeared in *The Eye-Beaters* [1970], and James Scully's "Letter from Windham Hospital," which appeared in his first volume, *Avenue of the Americas* [1971], and contains such passages as the following:

> Nurse's aide massages my back, motherly as a whirlpool bath
> she tucks us in
>   pyjamas and slippers
> like leftovers from Father's Day.
> Who wants to live that way?
> We're all grown men. . . .
> At night I wake up
>   bathed in sweat
> Joyful, like an athlete in an epic
>   drying out
> Between bouts of the most lavish funeral games.[6]

The danger of the Lowell mode—a danger from which Lowell himself, as I have argued earlier, is not always exempt, especially in his later poetry—is that the poem too easily becomes self-indulgent confession on the one hand or random description of objects on the other. The special strength of a poem like "Waking in the Blue" is that Lowell manages to mediate between self and world, personal response and external reality, consistently endowing the particular detail with typicality and universality. But in the "hospital poems" of Lowell's contemporaries and followers such mediation between self and world, the "I" and the other, is rarely found. Take, for example, John Berryman's "The Hell Poem," the first of a six-poem sequence in *Love and Fame* [1970] which explores the poet's confinement in and subsequent release from a mental hospital in the Midwest:

The Hell Poem

Hospital racket, nurses' iron smiles.
Jill & Eddie Jane are the souls.
I like nearly all the rest of them too
except when they feed me paraldehyde.

Tyson has been here three heavy months;
heroin. We have the same doctor: She's improving,
let out on pass tonight for the first time.
A madonna's oval face with wide dark eyes.

Everybody is jolly, patients, nurses,
orderlies, some psychiatrists. Anguishes;
gnawings. Protractions of return
to the now desired but frightful outer world.

Young Tyson hasn't eaten since she came back.
She went to a wedding, her mother harangued her
it was all much too much for her
she sipped wine with a girl-friend, she fled here.

Many file down for shock & can't say after
whether they ate breakfast. Dazed till four.
One word is: the memory will come back.
Ah, weeks or months. Maybe.

Behind the locked door, called 'back there',
the worse victims.
Apathy or ungovernable fear
cause them not to watch through the window starlight.

They can't have matches, or telephone. They slob food.
Tantrums & the suicidal, are put back there.
Sometimes one is promoted here. We are ecstatic.
Sometimes one has to go back.

It's all girls this time. The elderly, the men,
of my former stays have given way to girls,
fourteen to forty, raucous, racing the halls,
cursing their paramours & angry husbands.

Nights of witches: I dreamt a headless child.
Sobbings, a scream, a slam.
Will day glow again to these tossers, and to me?
I am staying days.[7]

According to the dust jacket, *"Love and Fame* is written in a style new for Berryman, new for anybody." It is true that Berryman has here discarded the peculiar and sometimes irritating syntactic dislocations and stylistic mannerisms of *The Dream Songs;* the style of *Love and Fame* is generally straightforward, idiomatic and "natural." This is not to say, however, that it is "new for anybody," for the ghost of Lowell surely lurks in the wings of Berryman's sanatorium. All the surface features of "Waking in the Blue" are here: the presentation of the poet as a "patient" who is at once very much like his fellow inmates and yet beyond them in his clear-headed perception of his malaise, the pained awareness that some people will stay here forever, the paradoxical fear of and longing for the outside world, the empathy for certain patients, the distrust of the "jolly" good humor of the nurses, orderlies, and psychiatrists, and the contempt for the meaningless daily hospital routine. As in the case of "Waking," the idiom is casual and colloquial, the verse free within set limits: the poem's thirty-six lines are divided into nine four-line stanzas, made up of four or five-stress lines that are organized via alliteration ("*S*obbings, a *s*cream, a *s*lam"), assonance ("cursing their p*a*ramours & *a*ngry husb*a*nds"), and consonance in place of end rhyme as in "*smiles*" / "*souls*" of lines 1–2.

Yet there is a basic difference between the two poems. Lowell's "I" is a participant in the morning ritual at McLean's; "Waking in the Blue" charts his experience during a particular time span, as he moves toward some measure of self-insight and understanding. The "I" of Berryman, by contrast, is usually a camera, recording what he perceives in the sanatorium as so much raw data: "hospital racket," her-

oin addiction, shock therapy, the dangerous ward, the predominance of female patients. The description of Tyson, the
young lesbian with a "madonna's oval face," turned heroin
addict, is painful in the way that a newspaper account or
photograph of such a girl would be painful, but it is not
really related to the other items in the poem. Whereas Lowell builds up a complex web of images, placing himself and
his companions in a precisely delineated landscape, Berryman simply tells about the hospital. Thus he likes Jill and
Eddie Jane and sympathizes with those who have been on
the dangerous ward, but he dislikes the nurses with their
"iron smiles" and is bothered by the frightening sounds that
punctuate the night. There is no metonymic linkage of images here: Jill and Eddie Jane could just as well be Joan and
Andy Sue, and the fact that "It's all girls this time" doesn't
really make much difference to the poet or, for that matter, to
the reader. Berryman's people, in short, are neither individ-
uals nor types—they are simply stereotypes: the young heroin addict whose face still has vestiges of innocent beauty,
the anguished poet, the "dangerous cases" who are deprived
of "matches, or telephone," the robot-like nurses.

Despite its clipped and racy speech ("Tyson has been here
three heavy months; / heroin" or "They slob food"), "The
Hell Poem" deals chiefly in abstractions: "Protractions of
return / to the now desired but frightful outer world," or
"Apathy or ungovernable fear / cause them not to watch
through the window starlight." When these abstractions are
reenforced by more concrete detail, the effect is generally arbitrary: the girls race the halls "cursing their paramours &
angry husbands"; Tyson is let out on pass only to quarrel
with her mother who makes her lesbian daughter go to a
wedding, and the dangerous patients are, predictably
enough, "Behind the locked door."

The arbitrariness of detail is reflected in the arbitrary use
of syntax. Berryman switches back and forth between simple

scussed in Chapter Two, the self is projected outward; it
ems to utter rather than to address anyone; it can recount
ly what is happening *now*, at this very moment.[12] A con-
uous present replaces Lowell's circular movement from
sent to past and back to the present.

But Plath's present, unlike Berryman's, is never merely
ic. "The Stones" may be usefully glossed by R. D. Laing's
unt of petrifaction in *The Divided Self* as "the dread
of the possibility of turning, or being turned, from a
person into a dead thing, into a stone, into a robot, an
omaton, without personal autonomy of action, an *it* with-
subjectivity." [13] Thus the poem charts the process
reby the self moves through death by petrifaction to the
cult moment of rebirth. At the beginning, the speaker
on a great anvil, waiting for the hammer strokes (in real-
he shock therapy) that will break down her old identity.
he sky flies out of sight "like the hat of a doll," she be-
s first "a still pebble" and then a vessel that contains a
e stone world, a "city of spare parts," a graveyard, "The
stone quiet, jostled by nothing." The doctors and
s are surrealistically transformed into dwellers of this
stone city who treat the poet as a dead object. Thus, as
reatment ends, the doctor becomes the "jewelmaster"
'drives his chisel to pry / Open one stone eye." Upon
ening, the poet is still stone, her lips "flint." But she
perceives her body as stitched together with "catgut"
he frozen world around her begins to dissolve. Finally,
ody becomes a "vase" which "houses / the elusive
Gradually, in other words, the patient is brought back
. She becomes aware of her "Ten fingers" shaping a
of shadows. Her mendings now "itch"—she can *fee*
hore.

The Stones," the self is not defined in terms of meto
objects and settings; rather, Plath uses the centra
or of petrifaction to give us a series of metamo

declarative sentences ("We have the same doctor," "Many
file down for shock," "She went to a wedding") and fragments like "Ah, weeks or months. Maybe," or "Sobbings, a
scream, a slam." It is not really clear why the speaker will
say, on the one hand, "They can't have matches, or telephone. They slob food," and on the other, "Anguishes,
gnawings," except to say that we all do switch back and forth
from complete sentences to fragments in this way when we
talk. "The Hell Poem" does not, in short, go far beyond the
raw data of experience; the speech resembles that of a casual
letter to a friend or a telephone call. The poet's anguish does
evoke a sort of stock response in us—the pathos we feel
when we see pictures of drug rehabilitation centers on the
TV screen—but the world of the poem is peculiarly one-dimensional.

Reading Berryman's mental hospital sequence with its references to "Revelations every two hours on the Lounge,"
and its rather platitudinous insistence that "Many of the
sane / walking the streets like trees / are weirder than my
mournful fellow-patients" (p. 77), one begins to wonder if
the confessional mode is not already losing its momentum.
The future direction of poetry, I think, lies elsewhere. To
understand the peculiar transformation that the Lowell
mode is currently undergoing, we must look, not to Berryman, or W. D. Snodgrass, or Anne Sexton, but to the poetry
of Sylvia Plath.

It is, of course, customary to link Plath to Lowell,[8] and
she herself said in an interview, "I've been very excited by
what I feel is the new breakthrough that came with, say,
Robert Lowell's *Life Studies*. This intense breakthrough
into very serious, very personal emotional experience, which
I feel has been partly taboo. Robert Lowell's poems about
his experiences in a mental hospital, for example, interest
me very much." [9] But although Sylvia Plath obviously ab-
sorbed much of Lowell's subject matter, she transformed it

into something quite different. Consider, for example, "The Stones" (1959), written the summer after Sylvia Plath had studied poetry with Lowell at Boston University. The poem is about the speaker's reaction to electro-shock therapy in the mental hospital.[10]

The Stones

This is the city where men are mended.
I lie on a great anvil.
the flat blue sky-circle

Flew off like the hat of a doll
When I fell out of the light. I entered
The stomach of indifference, the wordless cupboard.

The mother of pestles diminished me.
I became a still pebble.
The stones of the belly were peaceable,

The head-stone quiet, jostled by nothing.
Only the mouth-hole piped out,
Importunate cricket

In a quarry of silences.
The people of the city heard it.
They hunted the stones, taciturn and separate,

The mouth hole crying their locations.
Drunk as a fetus
I suck at the paps of darkness.

The food tubes embrace me. Sponges kiss my lichens away.
The jewelmaster drives his chisel to pry
Open one stone eye.

This is the after-hell: I see the light.
A wind unstoppers the chamber
Of the ear, old worrier.

The Artist as M

Water mollifies the flint lip,
And daylight lays its sameness on the
The grafters are cheerful,

Heating the pincers, hoisting the de
A current agitates the wires
Volt upon volt. Catgut stitches my f

A workman walks by carrying a pin
The storerooms are full of hearts.
This is the city of spare parts.

My swaddled legs and arms smell s
Here they can doctor heads, or an
On Fridays the little children com

To trade their hooks for hands.
Dead men leave eyes for others.
Love is the uniform of my bald n

Love is the bone and sinew of m
The vase, reconstructed, houses
The elusive rose.

Ten fingers shape a bowl for sh
My mendings itch. There is not
I shall be good as new.[11]

To move from "Waking in th
shift from a world of concrete
events to one of pure being. The
veals the difference:

This is the city where men are

I lie on a great anvil.

I became a still pebble.

Sylvia Plath's "I," unlike Lowel
attributes or surroundings. Rat

phoses in which the "I" constantly shifts identities. The un-peopled landscape of the poem has no mimetic reference; it is a projection of the poet's unconscious state. As a seer, the "I" cannot detach itself sufficiently to describe the real world outside itself; the poet can only call up the concrete images that objectify her shifting emotions.

The tensions in "The Stones" is thus not between self and world as it is in Lowell and, at least diagramatically, in Ber-ryman's "Hell Poem," but between what Richard Howard has aptly called "the lithic impulse—the desire to reduce the demands of life to the unquestioning acceptance of a stone —and the impulse to live on." [14] This kind of tension be-tween two conflicting unconscious drives distinguishes Plath's poetry from the documentary autobiographical mode of Lowell. In her mental hospital there is no room for "May-flower screwballs" for the simple reason that no one is there besides herself. The sense of person, place, and time is ab-sent; there is only an "I" undergoing what Rimbaud called "le dérèglement de tous les sens." Indeed, Sylvia Plath's tra-dition is that of Rimbaud and, more immediately, of Roethke, whose poetry, as Ted Hughes points out, she was studying closely at the time that she composed "The Stones." [15] It is the tradition of oracular or visionary poetry, the poetry of animistic projection in which "Je est un autre." In the more exciting new poetry of the seventies—in the work, say, of Jon Silkin or Galway Kinnell—the Plath idiom is becoming increasingly obsessive.

Perhaps, in ten or twenty years, we will consider Lowell's rhetoric a fairly conservative one. As Rimbaud's drunken boat is more and more frequently endowed with the status of archetypal modern voyager, we may well have fewer journeys made in those Tudor Fords and little black Chevies which Lowell has made such an authentic part of our poetic land-scape. I would posit, in short, that Lowell's direct influence, now at its height, will begin to decline in the later seventies.

Nevertheless, Lowell surely remains our outstanding poet of midcentury, the representative lyric historian of the era between 1945, the end of World War II, and the antinomian and self-consciously anarchic future, when the derangement of the senses which Rimbaud proclaimed as the poet's goal more than a hundred years ago, may well have become the norm of lyric poetry.

Notes

Preface

1. Louis L. Martz, review of *Notebook 1967–68* (the first edition) in *Yale Review*, 69 (1970), 254. Cf. Jerome Mazzaro, "Sojourner of the Self," *Nation*, 7 July 1969, p. 22.

2. "Registering the Awful Events," *Times Literary Supplement*, 25 Dec. 1970, p. 1514. An even harsher judgment is that of David Bromwich, "Reading Robert Lowell," *Commentary*, 52 (Aug. 1971), 81–83.

It is interesting to note that, even before the appearance of *Notebook*, British critics gave Lowell a much cooler reception than did their American counterparts. See Michael Fried, "The Achievement of Robert Lowell," *London Magazine*, n.s. 1 (Oct. 1962), 54–64; John Bayley, "Robert Lowell: The Poetry of Cancellation," *London Magazine*, 6 (June 1966), rpt. in *Robert Lowell: A Portrait of the Artist in His Time*, ed. Michael London & Roberts Boyers (New York: David Lewis, 1970), pp. 187–198; and Gabriel Pearson, "Lowell's Marble Meanings," in *The Survival of Poetry*, ed. Martin Dodsworth (London: Faber and Faber, 1970), pp. 56–99.

3. "On Stanley Kunitz' 'Father and Son,'" in *The Contemporary Poet as Artist and Critic*, ed. Anthony Ostroff (Boston: Little, Brown, 1964), p. 71.

Chapter One. "The Unforgivable Landscape":
The Nexus of Images

1. In "A Symposium on 'Skunk Hour,'" in *The Contemporary Poet as Artist and Critic*, ed. Anthony Ostroff (Boston: Little,

Brown, 1964), Lowell says, "I felt that the best style for poetry was none of the many poetic styles in English but something like the prose of Chekhov or Flaubert" (p. 108). See also Lowell's *Paris Review* interview in *Writers at Work: The Paris Review Interviews, Second Series,* ed. M. Cowley (New York: Viking, 1963), p. 350.

2. It is generally held that Lowell's early poetry is inferior to that of *Life Studies* (1959) and subsequent volumes. See, for example, Irvin Ehrenpreis, "The Age of Lowell," in *American Poetry,* Stratford-upon-Avon Studies 7, ed. Irvin Ehrenpreis (New York: St. Martins, 1965), rpt. in Thomas Parkinson, ed., *Robert Lowell, A Collection of Critical Essays,* Twentieth-Century Views (Englewood, N.J.: Prentice Hall, 1968), pp. 74–98. This collection of essays is subsequently noted as *TCV.* See also Gabriel Pearson, "Lowell's Marble Meanings," in *The Survival of Poetry,* ed. Martin Dodsworth (London: Faber and Faber, 1970), p. 63.

On the other hand, certain critics feel that Lowell has not lived up to his early promise. See Jerome Mazzaro, *The Poetic Themes of Robert Lowell* (Ann Arbor: University of Michigan Press, 1965), pp. 88ff.; Thomas Parkinson, *"For the Union Dead,"* in *TCV,* pp. 143–151.

Phillip Cooper's *The Autobiographical Myth of Robert Lowell* (Chapel Hill: University of North Carolina Press, 1970) is the one study that argues that Lowell's work is "unusually unified, as a body." The unifying principle is, according to Cooper, a "radical thematic ambivalence" with its "correlative formal principle, ambivalence as lyric structure" (p. 4). It is difficult to see how such *ambivalence*—a term reminiscent of Allen Tate's "tension" or Cleanth Brooks' "language of paradox"—is in any way uniquely characteristic of Lowell, and in fact Cooper's book is primarily devoted to source study and explication.

3. *Writers at Work,* p. 352.

4. "Symposium on 'Skunk Hour,'" p. 107.

5. The reader will notice that most of the references in this chapter are to four of Lowell's books: *Lord Weary's Castle* (1946), *Life Studies* (1959), *For the Union Dead* (1964), and *Notebook* (1970). It seemed superfluous to include Lowell's first volume of poetry, *Land of Unlikeness* (Cummington, Mass.: The Cummington Press, 1944), since this limited edition (250 copies) is out of print, and since a third of its poems reappear in *Lord*

Weary's Castle. Both *Mills of the Kavanaughs* (1951) and *Near the Ocean* (1967) are problematic transitional volumes, containing a small number of poems. Accordingly, I cite examples from these texts only occasionally. Because *Imitations* (1961) is wholly devoted to translations, however free, of the work of other poets, it is peripheral to this chapter; I shall consider Lowell's achievement as a translator in Chapter Two. In the case of the two *Notebooks—Notebook 1967–68* (1969) and *Notebook* (1970)—I generally refer to the revised and expanded second version, although in a few instances I use the earlier text in order to make a particular point. This is by no means a value judgment: Lowell scholars of the future will have to decide which of the two versions is the more adequate, and I suspect that most will agree with the *Times Literary Supplement* reviewer (see Preface, note 2) that the first version is less prolix, contains less careless writing, and has a more orderly overall structure. However, the 1970 text has the great advantage of being the more readily available paperback text.

6. The *Collected Poems of Wallace Stevens* (New York: Knopf, 1961), p. 534.

7. "Fall Weekend at *Milgate*," no. 3, in "Excerpt from 'The Dolphin,'" *The Review*, no. 26 (Summer 1971), p. 4. Sonnets from this series (*Review*, pp. 3–9) are subsequently referred to as *Dolphin*.

8. See *Romantic Image* (New York: Vintage, 1964), pp. 92–103.

9. Gabriel Pearson, for example, finds a "certain perversity" in the poem's conclusion: see *The Survival of Poetry*, p. 92.

10. This poem is discussed more fully in Chapter Five.

11. "In the Cage" reappears with minor changes in the *Notebooks*. All capital letters, except in lines 1 and 7, have been excised, and line 6 becomes "canaries sing the bars, and scream" in *Nbk 67* (p. 32) and "canaries chip the bars, and scream" in *Nbk* (p. 61).

12. "Age of Lowell," *TCV*, p. 97.

13. For example, in *Robert Lowell: The First Twenty Years* (New York: Farrar, Straus, 1962), p. 75, Hugh Staples comments that "To Delmore Schwartz" is "little more than a *jeu d'esprit*—a whimsical footnote to his [Lowell's] autobiography." Similarly, Jerome Mazzaro writes, "All in all it is the weakest poem of the

section [i.e., section iii of *Life Studies*]. The emphasis it places on clarity, the accurate and unmistakable exactness of its language, and the devices of foreknowledge and whimsy are not enough to rescue it wholeheartedly from bathos or mere personal anecdote (*Poetic Themes,* p. 102).

14. The reference is to lines 48–49 of "Resolution and Independence": "We poets in our youth begin in gladness; / But thereof come in the end despondency and madness."

15. Randall Jarrell observes that "The people too often seem to be acting *in the manner of* Robert Lowell, rather than plausibly as real people act" ("From the Kingdom of Necessity" *Poetry and the Age* [New York: Knopf, 1953], rpt. in London & Boyers, p. 40). Similarly, Herbert Leibowitz writes, "I do not think that the poems succeed mainly because Lowell cannot disguise his voice (or construct a persona)" ("Ancestral Voices," *Salmagundi,* 1 [Fall–Winter 1966–1967], rpt. London & Boyers, p. 211).

16. *Hudson Review,* 12 (Autumn 1959), rpt. London & Boyers, p. 58.

17. The phrase is that of Herbert Leibowitz; see note 15 above.

18. London & Boyers, p. 23.

19. "The Eye of the Storm," *Partisan Review,* 32 (Spring 1965), rpt. London & Boyers, pp. 61–62.

20. *Studies in Human Time,* trans. Elliott Coleman (Baltimore: Johns Hopkins University Press, 1956), pp. 350–354.

21. Preface to *The Aspern Papers, The Art of the Novel,* ed. R. P. Blackmur (New York: Scribner's, 1934), p. 164.

22. See Jay Martin, *Robert Lowell, University of Minnesota Pamphlets on American Writers,* no. 92 (Minneapolis: University of Minnesota Press, 1970), p. 29.

23. See dust jacket of *Notebook 1967–68,* verso.

Chapter Two. *The Limits of Imitation:*
Robert Lowell's Rimbaud

1. *Imitations,* p. xi. In an interview with D. S. Carne-Ross in 1968, Lowell said: "In a way the whole point of translation—of my translation anyway—is to bring into English something that didn't exist in English before," *Delos,* 1 (1968), 173.

2. London *Observer,* 14 March 1965, 26; rpt. on bookjacket of *Imitations.*

3. *The New Yorker,* 2 June 1962, 118–128; rpt. on bookjacket of *Imitations.*

4. "Four Poets and Others," *Minnesota Review,* 2 (1962), 403; "The Age of Lowell," *TCV,* p. 93. The view that *Imitations* should be read as an organized sequence on the model of *Life Studies* is also argued by Daniel Hoffman in "Robert Lowell's *Near the Ocean:* The Greatness and Horror of Empire," *The Hollins Critic,* 4 (Feb. 1967), 4–5. Hoffman views the sequence as "an exploration of Europe" in which Lowell comes to terms with his "spiritual forebears in other languages"; *Imitations* is "a long, fragmented poem of the self, struggling in its engagements with history." In the same vein, Richard J. Fein discusses the sequence's unifying themes—e.g., war, the quest, the "compassionate self"—in his *Robert Lowell* (New York: Twayne, 1970), pp. 72–92.

Ehrenpreis, Hoffman, and Fein convincingly argue that Lowell intended *Imitations* to be read as a sequence, but I would add that even a sequence must be composed of individually coherent parts. Certainly *Life Studies* is such a sequence.

5. The phrase is George Steiner's: see *Language and Silence* (New York: Atheneum, 1967), p. 215.

6. "Abuse of Privilege: Lowell as Translator," *Hudson Review,* 20 (1967–1968); rpt. in London & Boyers, p. 141. For similarly hostile reviews of *Imitations,* see Charles Chadwick, "Meaning and Tone," *Essays in Criticism,* 13 (1963), 432–435; Roger Hecht, "Rilke in Translation," *Sewanee Review,* 71 (1963), 513–522; Henry Gifford, "Review of *Imitations,*" *Critical Quarterly,* 5 (Spring 1963), 94–95.

7. *Hudson Review,* p. 91.

8. "Robert Lowell: The Poetry of Cancellation," *London Magazine,* 6 (June 1966); rpt. in London & Boyers, p. 197.

9. "The Trying Out of Robert Lowell," *Sewanee Review,* 72 (1964), 133.

10. "Age of Lowell," pp. 94–95. The adaptations of Rimbaud are found on pp. 74–92 of *Imitations.* More space is devoted to Rimbaud than to any other poet except Baudelaire, who receives twenty-eight pages.

11. *La Vie de Rimbaud et de son oeuvre* (Paris: Mercure de France, 1923), p. 86. "We have here the scene of rupture between Frederic and Vitalie. A rupture motivated by their total disagreement about the children." (This translation and subsequent ones in the Notes are mine.)

12. *Rimbaud* (Chicago: Phoenix Books, 1967), pp. 16–20.

13. See, for example, W. M. Frohock, *Rimbaud's Poetic Practice: Image & Theme in the Major Poems* (Cambridge, Mass.: Harvard University Press, 1963), pp. 144–151; Yves Bonnefoy, *Rimbaud par lui-même, Ecrivains de toujours* (Paris: Seuil, 1968), p. 73.

14. René Etiemble et Y. Gauclère, *Rimbaud,* new edition (Paris: Gallimard, 1950), p. 163. "The theme is the course of a river which reflects in succession different lights and surfaces."

15. *Rimbaud,* pp. 16–20.

16. The syntax of the third line is troublesome; the line may mean either that the silk is the color of white lilies or that it is embroidered with lilies. The reference to "quelque pucelle" in line 4 suggests that Rimbaud had medieval banners bearing the *fleur de lis* in mind.

17. Rimbaud, *Oeuvres,* ed. Suzanne Bernard (Paris: Garnier, 1960), p. 447.

18. The cruxes are discussed by Bernard in her critical edition, pp. 446–448. To give one example: "Les roses des roseaux" in line 38 has been interpreted in a variety of ways; it cannot be read literally, since reeds do not have roses. Bernard writes, "Suivant Delahaye, *les roses des roseaux* sont les fleurs des joncs. On peut penser aussi aux teintes roses données aux roseaux par le coucher du soleil, mais qui disparaissent ensuite, *devorées* par le crépuscule" (p. 447). "Following Delahaye, *the roses of the reeds* are the flowers of the reeds. One can also think of the rosy tints given to the reeds by the sunset, but which faded afterwards, *devoured* by the twilight."

19. Richard, *Poésie et Profondeur* (Paris: Seuil, 1955), p. 212. "The Rimbaldian paradise . . . is the watered earth, the porous ground. And one can understand, therefore, why Rimbaud is so extremely sensitive to all the forms of emergence of the liquid element, why he is so partial to substances—mud, moss, grass— which can absorb deep water and carry it to the surface until it

becomes clearly visible. It is porousness which permits the break-through."

20. See Richard, pp. 199–211, for discussion of these images.

21. "The study of Rimbaud's lapidary indicates clearly that, in fact, his geology contains a botany, that for him, the stone represents a fruit, a living product of the earth: just as in the case of flowers, he chose above all to visualize the act of flowering, so in the case of stone, he conjures up the hidden processes of genesis."

22. Like "Mémoire," "Nostalgia" has forty lines divided into five sections, each of which has two four-line stanzas. Lowell's imitation is thus a line-by-line rendition of Rimbaud's text. The substitution of blank verse stanzas for Rimbaud's alternately rhyming alexandrines is not a major change, since blank verse is in English poetry what the rhyming alexandrine is in French—the most common verse form. Both poets use frequent caesurae and run-on lines. Totally different, however, is the qualitative sound structure of the two poems; a whole essay might be devoted to this topic. Rimbaud uses the most elaborate vowel harmony, complex assonance, and internal rhyme, whereas Lowell uses many voiceless stops and fricatives, creating a harsh sound pattern. Notice the difference between "*L'*eau *cl*aire; *comme le sel* des *l*armes d'*en*fance," and "The *suck*ing ri*ver* wa*s* the child'*s salt* tears." Rimbaud's liquids, nasals, and open *e*'s and *a*'s are replaced by Lowell's *k, t, s,* and *z* sounds and the dominant vowel sound of *schwa* (ə).

23. "Towards Defining An Age of Sensibility," in *Fables of Identity, Studies in Poetic Mythology* (New York: Harcourt Brace, 1963), pp. 130–137.

24. See D. S. Carne-Ross, "The Two Voices of Translation," *TCV,* pp. 166–169; Ben Belitt, *"Imitations:* Translation as Personal Mode," *Salmagundi,* 1 (1966–1967); rpt. London & Boyers, pp. 120–126.

25. The text used is the bilingual Rimbaud: *Complete Works, Selected Letters,* trans. Wallace Fowlie (Chicago: Phoenix Books, 1967), pp. 122–125.

Chapter Three. *The Confessional Mode: Romanticism and Realism*

1. See Victor Erlich, *Russian Formalism: History, Doctrine,* 2d. rev. ed. (the Hague: Mouton, 1965), p. 202.

2. Donald Sheehan, "An Interview with James Merrill," *Contemporary Literature,* 9 (Winter 1968), 1–2.

3. *Writers at Work,* p. 349.

4. *The New Poets: American and British Poetry since World War II* (New York: Oxford, 1967), p. 15.

5. A. R. Jones defines the confessional poem as a "dramatic monologue in which the *persona* is naked ego involved in a very personal world and with particular, private experiences" ("On Necessity and Freedom: The Poetry of Robert Lowell, Sylvia Plath, and Anne Sexton," *Critical Quarterly,* 7 [1965], 14). Ralph J. Mills, Jr., defines confessional poetry as that which deals with "the more intimate aspects of life, areas of experience that most of us would instinctively keep from public sight" (*Contemporary American Poetry* [New York: Random House, 1965], p. 156).

6. "Confession and Equilibrium: Robert Lowell's Poetic Development," *Criticism,* 11 (Winter 1969), 79. See also Judson Jerome, *Poetry: Premeditated Art* (Boston: Houghton Mifflin, 1968), p. 347: "[*Life Studies*] seems to me a breakthrough from poetry into case study."

7. Lowell writes, "This is not my diary, my confession, not a puritan's too literal pornographic honesty, glad to share private embarrassment, and triumph" (*Nbk 67,* 159). Interestingly, in the 1970 text he prefaces this sentence with the remark that *Notebook* "is less an almanac than the story of my life," thus admitting the autobiographical impulse (*Nbk,* 262).

8. *Writers at Work,* p. 347.

9. "Poetry Since Yeats: An Exchange of Views," *TriQuarterly,* 4 (1965), 101–102.

10. "Structure and Style in the Greater Romantic Lyric," *From Sensibility to Romanticism: Essays Presented to Frederick A. Pottle,* ed. Frederick W. Hilles and Harold Bloom (New York: Ox-

ford, 1965), pp. 527–528. See also Robert Langbaum's definition of the "dramatic lyric" in *The Poetry of Experience* (New York: Norton, 1957), pp. 1–74.

11. *Romantic Image,* chap. 5 *passim.*

12. *Writers at Work,* p. 346.

13. *Ibid.,* pp. 368, 343.

14. "Symposium on 'Skunk Hour,'" Ostroff, p. 108. Interestingly, James Merrill says almost the same thing in the *Contemporary Literature* interview: "I've enjoyed reading novels more often—or more profoundly—than I've enjoyed reading poems. . . . You hear a voice talking in prose, often a very delightful voice which can say all kinds of odd things. For me, to get something of that into poetry was a pleasure and even perhaps an object" (p. 4).

15. Perhaps Gabriel Pearson has the realistic convention in mind when he comments that in *Life Studies* "Lowell was not making his poetry more personal but depersonalizing his own life" ("Lowell's Marble Meanings," *Survival of Poetry,* p. 58). However, neither Pearson nor Phillip Cooper who builds his case for an "autobiographical myth" in Lowell's poetry on Pearson's statement, explain how Lowell's "depersonalizing" distinguishes his work from that of his fellow poets. Cooper goes so far as to align Lowell's technique with Eliot's: "I have heard it maintained that the real innovation in *Life Studies* was not so much to treat the everyday as to use the poet's own personal history as subject, *contra* Eliot's influential conception of the impersonality of poetry. But this is to take a very narrow view of Eliot's idea as well as of Lowell's poems. Eliot did not mean that the personal should be avoided, only that it should be transformed . . ." (*Autobiographical Myth of Robert Lowell,* pp. 38–39). But since there never has been a lyric poet who did not somehow "transform" his "personal life" into art, Cooper's conception of confessional poetry seems much too broad to be useful.

16. Wellek, "The Concept of Realism in Literary Scholarship," *Concepts of Criticism* (New Haven: Yale University Press, 1963), pp. 222–255; Levin, "Realism in Perspective," *The Gates of Horn: Five French Realists* (New York, 1963), pp. 24–83.

17. "Chance and Design in *Anna Karenina,*" in *The Disciplines of Criticism: Essays in Literary Theory, Interpretation and*

History Honoring René Wellek, ed. Peter Demetz et al. (New Haven: Yale University Press, 1968), pp. 325–26.

18. "The Metaphoric and Metonymic Poles," in Roman Jakobson and Morris Halle, *Fundamentals of Language* (The Hague: Mouton, 1956), p. 77.

19. *Ibid.,* p. 78.

20. Erlich, *Russian Formalism,* p. 206.

21. *Theory of Literature,* 3d ed. (New York: Harcourt, 1956), p. 195.

22. *Poetic Themes of Robert Lowell,* p. 113.

23. Although he argues from precisely the same Symbolist premise as does Mazzaro, Phillip Cooper comes to the opposite conclusion: he finds the confessional poetry just as recondite and multi-layered as the early work. See, for example, his discussion of mandala symbolism and the Buddhist mythology of the tortoise in the poem "Night Sweat" (*Autobiographical Myth,* pp. 93–96). His conclusion that the theme of the poem is rebirth, based on the argument that the noun "cycle" in the last line of the poem can also be read as a verb, has been explicitly denied by Lowell himself (see Cooper, p. 94).

24. *Anna Karenina,* trans. Constance Garnett (New York: Modern Library, 1930), p. 123.

25. In *Madame Bovary,* Flaubert employs similar metonymic shifts from a part of the body to the whole man. When Charles first meets Emma, he is surprised by the "whiteness of her fingernails. They were almond-shaped, tapering, as polished and shining as Dieppe ivories," *Madame Bovary,* trans. Francis Steegmuller (New York: Modern Library, 1957), p. 17. Later, when Emma is falling in love with Leon, she notices that "his fingernails were longer than those of most other inhabitants of Yonville. The clerk spent a great deal of time caring for them: he kept a penknife in his desk for the purpose" (p. 107). Leon is, in turn, irritated when he visits the Bovarys and sees Emma sewing like a *bonne bourgeoise:* "The cloth seemed to be roughening the tips of her fingers" (p. 118). Throughout the novel, elegant fingernails metonymically stand for the romantic longing and false illusions that bring Emma and Leon together.

26. *Anna Karenina,* p. 130.

27. See Chekhov, "In the Ravine," *Peasants and Other Stories,*

ed. Edmund Wilson (New York: Anchor Books, 1956), p. 312, for a similar example of metonymy. On the morning of Anisim's wedding, his father pays the dressmakers not with the money promised but with "tallow candles and tins of sardines." This payment epitomizes the duplicity and greed of the Tsybukins and foreshadows the victimization of the bride Lipa by her future in-laws.

George Eliot is also a master of this type of metonymic transfer. In *The Mill on the Floss,* for example, the possessors are repeatedly characterized by their possessions: Tom by his fishing rods, Aunt Pullet by her polished floors, and Mrs. Tulliver by her "best chany."

28. *Anna Karenina,* p. 227.

29. See Mazzaro, *Poetic Themes,* pp. 111–116; Joseph Bennett, "Two Americans, a Brahmin and the Bourgeoisie," *Hudson Review,* 12 (1959–1960); rpt. in London & Boyers, pp. 58–59.

30. In "A Symposium on 'Skunk Hour,'" Lowell says of Stanzas V and VI: "This is the dark night. I hoped my readers would remember John of the Cross's poem. My night is not gracious, but secular, puritan, and agnostical. An Existentialist night" (p. 107).

Chapter Four. *The "Life-Blood of a Poem":*
The Uses of Syntax

1. *Syntax in English Poetry, 1870–1930* (Berkeley: University of California Press, 1967), p. 10. Briefly, Baker's argument is that poets writing in English have altered the normal pattern of sentences in one of three ways: (1) by *elaboration*—adding lengthy clauses or numerous parallel modifiers; (2) by *dislocation*—arranging the fundamental units of a sentence in unusual sequences; or (3) by *fragmentation.* Modern poets, Baker argues, have increasingly shown a preference for the third way, the sentence fragment. This thesis accords with Donald Davie's view that the modern poet "abandons even the appearance of syntactical arrangement and merely juxtaposes images," and that "What is common to all modern poetry is the assertion or the assumption . . . that syntax in poetry is wholly different from syntax as

understood by logicians and grammarians," *Articulate Energy* (London: Routledge & Kegan Paul, 1955), p. 148. Lowell's poetry, which falls outside the period studied by Baker, does not fit into such a scheme. As I shall argue here, Lowell prefers both elaboration and dislocation to fragmentation.

2. *Collected Poems* (New York: Doubleday, 1966), p. 187.

3. *Ariel* (New York: Harper, 1966), p. 26.

4. On this point, see pages 85–86. As early as 1953, in a review entitled "The Prose Genius in Verse," Lowell praised Robert Penn Warren's *Brother to Dragons* for its assimilation of plot and character into a long poem, thus breaking the symbolist impasse with its "Mary and Martha division" of the aesthetic (poetry) and the ephemeral (prose): in this poem, Warren "most truly seems to approach the power of those writers one has always felt hovering about him, those poetic geniuses in prose, Melville and Faulkner. In Warren's case, it is the prose genius in verse which is so startling," *Kenyon Review,* 15 (Autumn 1953), 625.

5. "Memories of West Street" is written in free verse, but its norm is the iambic pentameter line as in "and sáw the Húdson River ónce a dáy." Lowell varies this base line in every possible way; in the first two lines, for example, the falling rhythm captures the lassitude and inertia of the "cured" poet:

Ónly teáching on Túesdays, ‖ bóok-wôrming
in pajámas frésh from the wásher êach mórning.

Occasional rhyme is used for ironic effect in many places: for example, "book-worm*ing*"/"morn*ing*"; "trash *cans*"/"young Republi*can*"; "Easter p*alm*"/"sheepish c*alm*"; "entangle*ments*"/"tene*ments*". Lowell also uses complex patterns of alliteration as in the line: "F*lab*by, *bal*d, *lobo*tomized," where the repetition of *l*'s, *b*'s, *d*'s, open *a*'s, and *o*'s creates the mental image of a "blob."

6. See William Arrowsmith, "A Monotony of Violence," *Hudson Review,* 4 (Winter 1952); rpt. in London & Boyers, p. 32.

7. Josephine Miles' thesis is that there are two basic kinds of sentence structure. "The first or phrasal type employs an abundance of adjectives and nouns, in heavy modification and compounding of subjects, in a variety of phrasal constructions, including verbs turned to participles; it is a cumulative way of

speaking. The second or clausal type emphasizes compound or se-
rial predicates, subordinate verbs in relative and adverbial
clauses, action, and rational subordination; it is a discursive way
of speaking" (*Eras and Modes in English Poetry* [Berkeley: University of California, Press, 1964), p. 2.

I follow Miles in counting participles as adjectives rather than
as verbs. "Adjectives include compared forms; verbs, all forms
but the participles, which, in disagreement with some modern
linguists, I take to be most significant in their adjectival, phrasal
functions. Indeed it is the substitution of such forms as *the blow-
ing wind* for *the wind which blows* that makes one of the main
differences between phrasal and clausal modes" (note to Table I,
p. 250).

8. Counting parts of speech in the first thousand lines of *Lord
Weary's Castle,* Miles finds the following proportions: adjectives
—740; nouns—2,130; verbs—1,010; or 7 : 21 : 10, a ratio characteristic of a balanced rather than a phrasal mode (p. 261).

9. "Randall Jarrell," in *Randall Jarrell, 1915–1965,* ed. Robert
Lowell, Peter Taylor, and Robert Penn Warren (New York:
Noonday, 1968), pp. 111–112.

10. I borrow this term from Maynard Mack, "Wit and Poetry
and Pope," in *Eighteenth-Century Literature,* ed. James Clifford
(New York: Oxford, 1959), p. 30.

11. See *Eras and Modes,* p. 261. These statistics refer to *LWC*
only; hence the high incidence of verbs.

12. It first appeared in the *Nation,* 53 (3 Aug. 1946), shortly
before its publication in book form. For a chronology of the
poems in *LWC,* see Hugh Staples, *Robert Lowell,* Appendix.

13. The source was first identified by G. Giovannini, *Explicator,* 9 (June 1951), item 53, and is reprinted in Mazzaro, *Poetic
Themes,* pp. 69–70.

14. For the possible symbolic significance of September 22 (the
feast day of St. Thomas of Villanova as well as the date of the
death of Persephone), see Mazzaro, *Poetic Themes,* p. 70.

15. The reference is, of course, to Kenyon College in Gambier,
Ohio, where Lowell first met Jarrell, but within the confines of
the poem the train ride is not endowed with sufficient significance to make it an integral part of the whole.

16. In attacking the rhetoric of *Notebook* (1970), the *Times*

Literary Supplement reviewer made a similar point: "Consider the three-adjective device, once surprising and supple, but now trundled out mechanically" (25 Dec. 1970), p. 1514.

Chapter Five. *The Voice of the Poet: The Winslow Elegies*

1. Roy Harvey Pearce, *The Continuity of American Poetry* (Princeton, N.J.: Princeton University Press, 1961), pp. 24–25.
2. Pearce, p. 29.
3. *Poetry and the Age* (New York: Knopf, 1953), p. 212.
4. Herbert Leibowitz writes, "Lowell excels at funerary art, at epitaph making. . . . The weight of his ancestors is heavy; they speak to him from the grave of loss" ("Ancestral Voices," London & Boyers, p. 202). See also Josephine Jacobsen, "Poet of the Particular," *Commonweal,* 81 (1964–1965), 345–350; Christopher Ricks, "The Three Lives of Robert Lowell," *New Statesman,* 69 (26 March 1965), 496. It is curious that although the prose autobiography "91 Revere Street" deals almost exclusively with Lowell's paternal relatives, the poetry of *Life Studies* concerns itself with the Winslows rather than the Lowells.
5. "The Age of Lowell," *TCV,* p. 92.
6. Many of the sonnets in *Notebook* also memorialize Lowell's Winslow relatives, even if they are too short to be considered full-fledged elegies. See, for example, "For Aunt Sarah" (p. 64), "Two Farmers" (p. 72), "Those Older" (p. 123), "Revenants" (p. 179).
7. See Leibowitz, p. 202; Ehrenpreis, p. 80. A minority view is voiced by Gabriel Pearson in "Lowell's Marble Meanings," *The Survival of Poetry,* pp. 59–60. Pearson writes, "It is hard to remember that this is a formal commemorative poem about a man whom Lowell reverenced. There seems to be an unacknowledged flight into the omnipotence of manic verbal control which conceals an impotence adequately to mourn" (p. 60).
8. *Poetic Themes of Robert Lowell,* pp. 7, 17.
9. *Robert Lowell: The First Twenty Years,* p. 29.
10. Cummington, Mass.: Cummington Press, 1944. Pages of introduction are unnumbered.
11. Whatever features an elegy may have, most critics would

agree that it must contain both lament and consolation. Stephen F. Fogle, for example, defines the genre as follows: "A lyric, usually formal in tone and diction, suggested either by the death of an actual person or by the poet's contemplation of the tragic aspects of life. In either case the emotion, originally expressed as a lament, finds consolation in the contemplation of some personal principle" (*Encyclopedia of Poetry and Poetics,* ed. Alex Preminger et al. [Princeton, N.J.: Princeton University Press, 1965], p. 215).

12. Since, as I explained in Chapter One, note 5, *Land of Unlikeness* is not readily available, the text used is the second version, which appeared in *Lord Weary's Castle* (pp. 19–22). There is a detailed comparison of the two versions, which are not essentially different, in Mazzaro, *Poetic Themes,* pp. 4–19.

13. See Mazzaro, *Poetic Themes,* pp. 12–13; Staples, pp. 28–29; Ralph Mills, Jr., "Robert Lowell," *Contemporary American Poetry* (New York: Random House, 1965), pp. 125–136.

14. The phrase is Denis Donoghue's (*Connoisseurs of Chaos: Ideas of Order in Modern American Poetry* [New York: Macmillan, 1965], p. 154).

15. For the Winslow background, see Mazzaro, *Poetic Themes,* p. 15; Phillip Cooper, *Autobiographical Myth of Robert Lowell,* p. 15.

16. "Some Aspects of Modern American Poetry," *The Complex Fate* (London: Chatto & Windus, 1952), p. 161.

17. See Apocalypse 18: 22. Mazzaro gives a detailed explication of this passage (pp. 16–18), and Staples locates the source of "The painted paradise of harps and lutes" in François Villon's "Ballade—Que Villon Feist à la Requeste de sa Mère Pour Prier Nostre Dame" (p. 98).

18. In the *Lord Weary's Castle* version, quotation marks surround the second stanza; Staples therefore concludes that the speaker here is Grandfather Winslow himself. The text does not, however, support such a reading: the "I" says that he finds "no painted idols to adore," whereas Arthur Winslow clearly does admire the "painted paradise." Moreover, the prayer to the Blessed Virgin ("Mother, run to the chalice") is perfectly consistent with the speaker's prayer in the first stanza. Staples' argument that the "lavabis *nos*" indicates a modulation to the voice of Arthur

Winslow (p. 9) is not convincing. The quotation marks are not the only sign of confusion in the second stanza; even Mazzaro, whose praise for the elegy is almost unqualified, notes that it makes no sense for the speaker to "strike for shore" when he has just said that he is "beached / On these dry flats of fishy real estate" (p. 19).

19. *Kenyon Review,* 7 (1945); rpt. in London & Boyers, p. 4.

20. See Staples, chapter 4 *passim;* Mazzaro, *Poetic Themes,* pp. 37–44; Leibowitz, pp. 207–209; Mills, pp. 141–144; Richard Fein, "Mary and Bellona: The War Poetry of Robert Lowell," *Southern Review,* 1 (1965), 826–831.

21. John Thompson writes, " 'The Quaker Graveyard,' for instance, is an elegy which may be compared at length and in detail with 'Lycidas' without suffering much at any point," *Kenyon Review,* 21 (1959), 485. See also Staples, pp. 45–52.

22. *John Milton: A Reader's Guide to his Poetry* (New York: Noonday, 1963), pp. 105–111. Marjorie Nicholson describes the structure as that of a sonata-symphony with an overture and three movements.

23. "Literature as Context: Milton's 'Lycidas,' " *Fables of Identity* (New York: Harbinger Books, 1963), p. 121. Frye writes, "The body of the poem is arranged in the form ABACA, a main theme repeated twice with two intervening episodes as in the musical rondo. The main theme is the drowning of Lycidas in the prime of life; the two episodes, presided over by the figures of Orpheus and Peter, deal with the theme of premature death as it relates to poetry and the priesthood respectively. . . . The most difficult part of the construction is the managing of the transitions from these episodes back to the main theme."

24. See Nicholson, *John Milton,* p. 106.

25. The imagery of this passage is taken from the opening chapter of Thoreau's *Cape Cod;* see Staples, p. 101.

26. Lowell himself points out his source in the Preface to *LWC;* for the full source, see Staples, pp. 103–104.

27. Staples believes that the expressionless face of Our Lady of Walsingham points toward "a state in which all human aspirations and concerns must be left behind," the state of mystical union with God" (p. 51).

28. Ehrenpreis makes an interesting comparison between this

passage and Eliot's *Four Quartets:* "If we compare Lowell's two stanzas, in their attempt to express the inexpressible, with similar passages in Eliot's 'Dry Salvages' . . . we must admit that there is a posed air, a willed simplicity, in Lowell's lines that never appears in, say, 'Lady, whose shrine stands on the promontory', etc." (p. 83). Cf. Gabriel Pearson, "Lowell's Marble Meanings," p. 64.

29. "Mary and Bellona," *Southern Review,* 868.

30. Even this supposedly affirmative image is ambiguous. The allusion is to *Paradise Lost,* I, 462–463; here Milton describes the fallen angels who arrive in Hell, having died for Mammon, as "Sea-monsters, upward angel, downward fish." The fallen angels, in other words, maintain some semblance of their former radiance even as they enter Hell. By analogy, it would seem that the "blue sailors" also enter Hell. Why, then, does the poet say, "It's well"?

31. "Uncle Devereux Winslow" is written in free verse paragraphs of varying length: the lines range from two stresses ("óne wínter") to six ("Whát were those súnflôwers? Púmpkins flóating shóulder-hígh?") and there is occasional rhyme as in "my Great Aunt Sar*ah*/was learning Samson and Delil*ah*").

32. See Richard Calhoun, *Explicator,* 23 (1965), item 38.

33. Yeats's stanza is $a_4b_3c_4b_3d_5d_3$—a ballad stanza plus an unequal couplet. Lowell's stanza has no fixed verse form: the lines range from two to six primary stresses and there is occasional rhyme as in "sc*reen*" / "ever*green*" and "Gyp*sy*" / "hap*py*". The following line, with its marked alliteration, assonance, internal rhyme, clustering of stresses, and caesurae is typical of the poem's appropriately slow and somewhat broken rhythm:

to the áir ‖ blásting ‖ an áll-whîte wáll ‖ whíter

34. "The Eye of the Storm," *Partisan Review,* 33 (1965); rpt. in London & Boyers, p. 62.

35. Compare, for example, the following passage from a slightly later poem, the miniature elegy "For Aunt Sarah" (Nbk 67, 34), to Stanzas V–VIII of "Fourth of July in Maine":

. . . in short a lady,
still reaching past the turn of the century

for your youth in that solid golden age, when means
needed only to follow the golden mean
to guide and enjoy the world; when business captains
and their crews of statesmen willingly gave up
health, wealth and pleasure from the stones of office,
guided by their only fiction, God.

36. "Robert Lowell and the Public Dimension," *Encounter*, 30 (April 1968), 76. See also Louis L. Martz, *Yale Review*, 56 (June 1967), 597: "[Lowell] is not at heart a satirist; he is a poet who at his best expresses an anguished, elegiac pity for suffering man. But the original poems in this book [*Near the Ocean*] too often tend to crush or disintegrate the sense of pity by gestures of cynicism and grinding images of misery."

Conclusion. *Lowell and Some Contemporaries:*
A Portrait of the Artist as Mental Patient

1. "Randbemerkungen zur Prosa des Dichters Pasternak," *Slavische Rundschau*, 7 (1935); rpt. in French translation as "Notes Marginales sur la prose du poète Pasternak," *Poétique*, 7 (1971), 319. My translation.

2. The phrase is Hegel's as cited by Georg Lukacs, who regards the "totality of objects" as a hallmark of realism; see *Studies in European Realism* (New York: Universal Library, 1964), p. 151.

3. "Structure and Style in the Greater Romantic Lyric," *From Sensibility to Romanticism*, p. 528.

4. *Writers at Work*, p. 345.

5. Rhyming units are circled and connected by lines. Alliterating consonants and assonantal vowels are underlined.

6. *Avenue of the Americas* (Amherst, Mass.: University of Massachusetts Press, 1971), p. 49.

7. *Love & Fame* (New York: Farrar, Straus & Giroux, 1970), pp. 73–74.

8. See especially, M. L. Rosenthal, *The New Poets*, chapters 2 and 3, passim; George Steiner, "Dying is an Art," *The Reporter*, 33, no. 6 (Oct. 7, 1965); rpt. in *The Art of Sylvia Plath*, ed. Charles Newman (London: Faber and Faber, 1970), p. 215;

A. R. Jones, "On Necessity and Freedom: The Poetry of Robert Lowell, Sylvia Plath, and Anne Sexton," *Critical Quarterly,* 7 (1965), 11–30. For a recent challenge to these views of the Lowell-Plath relationship, see Irving Howe, "Sylvia Plath: a Partial Disagreement," *Harper's,* Jan. 1972, pp. 89–91.

9. Cited by A. Alvarez, "Sylvia Plath," in *The Art of Sylvia Plath,* p. 62.

10. In his dating of Plath's poems, Ted Hughes suggests that "The Stones" was a major turning point in Plath's career: "She was reading Paul Radin's collection of African folktales with great excitement. In these, she found the underworld of her worst nightmares throwing up intensely beautiful adventures, where the most unsuspected voices thrived under the pressures of a reality that made most accepted fiction seem artificial and spurious. At the same time she was reading—closely and sympathetically for the first time—Roethke's poems. The result was a series of pieces, each a monologue of some character in an underground, primitive drama. STONES was the last of them. . . . It is full of specific detail of her experience in a mental hospital, and is clearly enough the first eruption of the voice that produced ARIEL. It is the poem where the self, shattered in 1953, suddenly finds itself whole" ("Notes on the Chronological Order of Sylvia Plath's Poems," *The Art of Sylvia Plath,* p. 192).

11. *The Colossus* (New York: Alfred A. Knopf, 1962), pp. 82–84.

12. I discuss this aspect of Plath's work more fully in my essay "Angst and Animism in the Poetry of Sylvia Plath," *Journal of Modern Literature,* 1 (first issue 1970), 57–74.

13. *The Divided Self* (1960; rpt. Baltimore Md.: Penguin Books, 1970), p. 46.

14. "Sylvia Plath: 'And I Have No Face. I Have Wanted to Efface Myself . . . ,'" in *The Art of Sylvia Plath,* p. 79.

15. See note 10.

Index of Lowell's Works

General Index

The Poetic Art of
Robert Lowell

Designed by R. E. Rosenbaum.
Composed by Vail-Ballou Press, Inc.,
in 11 point linofilm Baskerville, 2 points leaded,
with display lines in Deepdene.
Printed offset by Vail-Ballou Press
on P & S offset, 60 pound basis.
Bound by Vail-Ballou Press
in Columbia book cloth
and stamped in All Purpose foil.

Library of Congress Cataloging in Publication Data
(For library cataloging purposes only)

Perloff, Marjorie.
  The poetic art of Robert Lowell.

  Includes bibliographical references.
    1. Lowell, Robert, 1917-   I. Title.
PS3523.089Z82   811'.5'2   72-12412
ISBN 0-8014-0771-0